Dyslexia, Languages and Multilingualism.

Edited by Professor John Everatt
Managing Editor Liz Horobin.

Professor Usha Goswami's chapter is reproduced with kind permission from the author as first published in 2010 by Routledge.

Published by **The British Dyslexia Association.**
Unit 8 Bracknell Beeches, Old Bracknell Lane, Bracknell, RG12 7BW

Helpline: 0845-251-9002
Administration: 0845-251-9003
Website: **www.bdadyslexia.org.uk**

Cover design by Dianne Giblin.
www.diannegiblin.wordpress.com
thegiblins@hotmail.co.uk

LOTTERY FUNDED

The BDA gratefully acknowledges the Big Lottery Fund, the largest distributor of National Lottery good cause funding across the UK.
The Funds aim to enable others to make real improvements to communities and the lives of people most in need.

D0550931

ISBN 978-1-872653-62-4

9 781872 653624

British Dyslex!a
Association

Editorial Note.

The views expressed in this book are those of the individual contributors, and do not necessarily represent the policy of the British Dyslexia Association.

The BDA does not endorse the advertisements included in this publication.

Whilst every effort has been made to ensure the accuracy of information given in this handbook, the BDA cannot accept responsibility for the consequences of any errors or omissions in that information.

In certain articles the masculine pronoun is used purely for the sake of convenience.

Published in Great Britain 2012.
Copyright © British Dyslexia Association 2012.

Printed by Information Press, Eynsham, Oxford.
www.informationpress.com

Advertising sales by Space Marketing.
Tel: 01892-677-740
Fax: 01892-677-743
Email: **brians@spacemarketing.co.uk**

British Dyslexia Association.

Unit 8, Bracknell Beeches, Old Bracknell Lane, Bracknell RG12 7BW

Helpline: 0845-251-9002
Administration: 0845-251-9003
Fax: 0845-251-9005

Website: **www.bdadyslexia.org.uk**

BDA is a company limited by guarantee, registered in England No. 1830587

Registered Charity No. 289243

About the authors.

Nicola Brunswick BSc (Hons), Dip, PhD, PGCertHE is Senior Lecturer in psychology at Middlesex University, UK. She completed her PhD in the neuropsychology of dyslexia from the University of Warwick and her postdoctoral training at the Wellcome Department of Imaging Neuroscience and the MRC Cognitive Development Unit in London. She is a trustee of the British Dyslexia Association.

Jill Fernando is a project manager and trainer for the British Dyslexia Association. She is currently working on the EU funded project, Dyslang, which involves developing a course for teachers to support the multilingual dyslexic child to learn an additional curriculum language.

Usha Goswami is Professor of Cognitive Developmental Neuroscience at the University of Cambridge and a Fellow of St John's College, Cambridge. She is also Director of the Centre for Neuroscience in Education, which carries out research into the brain basis of literacy, numeracy, dyslexia and dyscalculia. Specific areas of interest include reading, dyslexia, phonological development and reasoning by analogy across languages. A major focus of current research is the brain basis of dyslexia and SLI, with funding from the MRC and Nuffield Foundation. She has received a number of career awards, including the British Psychology Society Spearman Medal, the Norman Geschwind-Rodin Prize for Dyslexia research, and BPS President's Award 2012, with Fellowships from the National Academy of Education (USA), the Alexander von Humboldt Foundation (Germany) and the Leverhulme Trust.

Dr Mim Hutchings, Senior Lecturer in Education Studies has developed undergraduate and masters modules on social and educational inclusion and language and literacy within Education Studies, PGCE and Masters programmes. Her current research is in dyslexia and multilingualism and narrative research in undergraduate learning. Her previous lives have included teaching in schools (nursery through to secondary) and universities, as an advisor for special educational needs and in ethnic minority support services.

Dr. Kathleen Kelly, Ph.D., M.Ed. (SEN), Dip. TESL, AMBDA is a Senior Lecturer at Manchester Metropolitan University where she is Programme Leader for the M.A. in Specific Learning Difficulties. She has wide experience of teaching courses on specific learning difficulties (dyslexia) at both undergraduate and postgraduate levels. She has many years' experience of supporting multi-lingual children with special educational needs (including dyslexia). Her doctorate was in the area of multilingualism and dyslexia.

Kathleen Kelly is Programme Leader for Specific Learning Difficulties (Dyslexia) at Manchester Metropolitan University.

Dr. Tilly Mortimore: Senior lecturer in Inclusion and SpLD/dyslexia

Tilly Mortimore joined Bath Spa from Southampton University in 2007 and has developed undergraduate modules and a successful Masters programme in SpLD/dyslexia. She currently researches dyslexia, inclusion and vulnerable learners and heads the research team in the Big Lottery funded project, Dyslexia and Multilingualism, in partnership with the British Dyslexia Association. She has taught and lectured in a range of international educational and training contexts including South Africa. Her recent publications include a second edition of "Dyslexia and Learning Style" and with Jane Dupree "Supporting Learners with SpLD/dyslexia in the Secondary Classroom".

Anny Northcote is a senior lecturer in Education Studies at Bath Spa University leading modules on reading and children's literature, as well as linguistic diversity in schools and communities. Before entering Higher Education she worked for many years in the east end of London as a primary teacher, language co-ordinator and advisor for bilingual children. She has published in areas of linguistic diversity and children's reading choices.

Sylvia Phillips, B.A., DASE, M.Ed. (SEN), AMBDA is an independent educational consultant in special educational needs. She currently leads postgraduate courses in dyslexia for Glyndwr University having formerly led such courses at Manchester Metropolitan University. Her teaching experience involved working in multilingual schools and she has a particular interest in this area.

Sylvia Phillips is an independent consultant in Special Educational Needs and Tutor to specialist courses at Glyndwr University.

Dr Ian Smythe is Visiting Professor at the School of Education, University of Wales, Newport, as well as an independent consultant. He writes extensively about dyslexia and assistive technology and is author of "Dyslexia in the Digital Age" published by Continuum. He has worked on more than ten multinational EU funded projects, and his current research interests include online multilingual assessment, comorbidity and computerisation of support.

He may be contacted at **ianssmythe@gmail.com**

Contents.

Foreword.

Populations are becoming more mobile, leading to sometimes dramatic changes in societies. These changes can lead to classrooms in which children speak a home/first language that is different from the language of education. In places of relatively large immigration, there may be a range of home/first languages spoken by children in a local school – in one, near to the University of Canterbury, New Zealand, over a dozen first languages were spoken by young children in a recent class, despite English being the only language spoken by their teacher. Furthermore, the importance of English as the current language of international business means that many countries are aiming for their children to be effective communicators in English. This has led to English being one of the languages of education in many countries, a second language in others and an important taught foreign language in still more, even if it is not a language used regularly outside of education. Therefore, teaching children in a language that may not be their first/ main language is a growing feature of modern schools.

The importance of supporting/including children with special educational needs (SEN) also is recognised as an important component of a modern educational system – United Nations education agreements are clear evidence of the position that SEN has acquired over the last couple of decades, at least in terms of policy. Dyslexia is clearly a part of this policy work; indeed, those advocating for dyslexia can claim an important contribution to this recognition. The primary educational feature of dyslexia (poor literacy acquisition) and the relationship between this feature and language (the written word is a representation of the language) mean that work in the dyslexia field should inform policy and practice related to supporting children learning within a second/additional language context. The work discussed in this publication is clear evidence of this role. That the British Dyslexia Association is supporting this work (e.g., the project reported by Mortimore and colleagues) is further confirmation of the involvement of the association in the forefront of such world-wide practices.

This publication combines a series of chapters written in different styles, which is probably consistent with work that, of necessity, covers a range of disciplines and expertise: some are written in a more research-based style, whereas others are more personal (Mortimore's *et al.*, versus Fernando's report of the same BDA-supported project shows this difference in style most clearly). However, all of the chapters reflect the dedication of professionals in the field to learn more about how to support children and adults with dyslexia/literacy-related learning difficulties. What the reading of this booklet will confirm also is that there is still a lot for us to learn about the relationship between language (particularly second/additional language acquisition) and literacy – although there is also a lot that we can do to support learning (see Mortimore *et al*'s discussion, but also Smythe's contribution). Areas for further work should become most evident when reading the chapter by Brunswick and the republication of the manuscript by Goswami. Both suggest how the relationship between features of the child's first and second language may influence literacy acquisition, which may make the assessment of literacy learning difficulties even more of a challenge than when identifying those with dyslexia in English – a problem clearly identified in the chapter by Phillips & Kelly. However, as comes across from the case study reported by Fernando, this can be as rewarding, and as important, as working with any group of children who may be struggling with dyslexia-related difficulties.

Therefore, I would like to commend the BDA for bringing together this group of chapters (and the other works in this 40th year celebratory series) and add my thanks for 40 years of indispensable, and continued successful, hard work.

John Everatt

Chapter 1 – Dyslexie, Legasthenie, Ordblindhed[1]: Dyslexia in different languages.

Dr Nicola Brunswick.

Much of what we know about how children learn to read, and about the difficulties of dyslexia, comes from studies conducted in English-speaking countries. Models of reading derived from this research are then often applied to speakers of other languages. But English is not a typical language. Over the centuries it has absorbed many words from other languages – for example, *assassin* (Arabic), *ballet* (French), *poltergeist* (German), *theory* (Greek), *alligator* (Spanish) – causing it to be inconsistent and unpredictable.

This atypicality has led some researchers to make unfounded assumptions about the nature of reading and dyslexia in other languages when those languages differ structurally from English. The complexity and consistency of different languages, and the effect that this has on reading and dyslexia, are considered below.

The complexity and consistency of language.

Languages may be broadly classified into two groups:

Those that have a consistent and predictable relationship between the spoken sounds of the language and the letters used to represent them. These languages are described as being 'transparent' or 'shallow', and examples include Italian, Finnish and Croatian.

---

1   The words used for dyslexia/wordblindness in French, German and Danish

Those that have an inconsistent and largely unpredictable relationship between the spoken sounds of the language and the letters used to represent them. These languages are described as being 'opaque' or 'deep', and examples include English and Danish.

In transparent languages there is an almost one-to-one relationship between the sounds of the spoken language and the written letters by which they are represented – i.e. most sounds can only be written in one way, and most letters can only be pronounced in one way. Once this relationship has been learned, reading and spelling skills develop rapidly; for example, Italian, Finnish and Croatian children are able to read and spell with almost 100 per cent accuracy after only a few months of instruction.

By contrast, in opaque languages there is a one-to-many relationship between the sounds of the spoken language and the written letters by which they are represented. For example, English is made up of 40 individual sounds which may be represented by around 1,120 possible letters or combinations of letters. Just think of the different ways in which the letters 'ough' are pronounced in the words *cough, hiccough, bough, through, thought,* and of the numerous ways that the 'o' sound can be written in the words *oh, go, sew, low, toe,* and *though* (not to mention the words *beau* and *faux* which have been assimilated into English from French).

It should be noted, however, that the story is not quite that clear. While Italian, Finnish and Croatian are transparent in terms of both their spelling and their reading, and English is opaque in terms of both its spelling and reading, some languages, such as Greek, are transparent for reading but rather opaque for spelling. In Greek each written letter may only be pronounced in one way, but three of the five vowel sounds may be written in more than one way. This results in young Greek children making rapid progress with their reading (similar to Italian children) but much slower progress with their spelling (similar to English children).

As even this brief overview of the structure and complexity of these different languages shows, the nature of the language can have a significant bearing on the ease with which its speakers learn to read and spell.

Learning to read in transparent and opaque languages.

Learning to read and spell in transparent languages is fairly straightforward. Instruction is based around mapping letters consistently onto the sounds of the spoken language, and even children with dyslexia can be taught effectively in this way. However, learning to read and spell in opaque languages requires considerable time and effort. In these languages children need to learn which words may be read and spelt reliably according to the basic spelling-sound rules of their language, and which may not.

The impact of a child's native language on their reading development has been demonstrated clearly by a large research project which assessed the reading skills of five to seven year old children from across Europe. The children were asked to read simple, familiar words from their own language (e.g. boat) and made-up words (e.g. bina). Reading made-up words requires children to apply their knowledge of the spelling-sound rules of their language as these words are unfamiliar so cannot be recognised by sight. This project tested over 500 children and found that by the end of the first year of schooling, reading accuracy for familiar words was almost perfect (greater than 90 per cent) in Finnish, Greek, Italian, Spanish, Swedish, Dutch, Icelandic, Norwegian and German-speaking children. It was around 70 to 80 per cent in French, Portuguese and Danish children, but only around 34 per cent in English-speaking children. These results reflect quite neatly the transparency of the languages for reading, from Finnish at the transparent end of the scale to English at the opaque end.

A similar pattern of results emerged for the reading of made-up words. By the end of the first year of school, Norwegian, Finnish, Greek and German-speaking children could read 90-95 per cent of the made-up words accurately. Italian, Spanish, Swedish, Dutch, Icelandic and French children could read 82-89 per cent of the words accurately, as could 77 per cent of Portuguese children. Danish children were 54 per cent accurate and English speaking children were 29 per cent accurate. Even by the end of the second school year, English-speaking children had still not caught up with most of their European counterparts from the year before, being able to read only 76 per cent of real words and 64 per cent of made-up words.

These findings indicate that the development of basic reading skills in English-speaking children occurs twice as slowly as in non-English-speaking European children. Once again, this might be predicted on the basis of the transparency and complexity of the languages. Children whose native languages are opaque and unpredictable experience much greater difficulty learning the spelling-sound rules of their languages than do children whose native languages are transparent and predictable.

Although English-speaking children are considerably slower at developing these basic reading skills than are non-English-speaking children, the good news is that they do catch up. While seven year old Finnish children are able to read with 90 per cent accuracy after around ten weeks of reading instruction, English-speaking children may achieve this level of accuracy after around four or five years. Differences in the reading ability of speakers of different languages have generally disappeared by the time they are 12 or 13 years old.

Dyslexia in transparent and opaque alphabetic languages.

Just as the ease with which children learn to read and spell depends on the transparency of their language, so does the incidence and manifestation of dyslexia. Around one to five percent of speakers of transparent languages are thought to be dyslexic, and this figure rises to around ten per cent for speakers of opaque languages. This is not due to any fundamental difference in the brains or genes of individuals from different countries.

If someone's physiological makeup has caused them to have difficulty with identifying and manipulating the sounds of language (i.e. they have impaired phonological awareness) then they will be dyslexic. If that person lives in a country that has a transparent language then they may not be aware of their difficulty and they may not be identified as being dyslexic. They may cope adequately with their daily reading since this is likely to be no less accurate than that of their non-dyslexic peers. However, if that same person lives in a country with an opaque language, then they will be far more likely to experience problems with their reading and spelling, and they will be more likely to be identified as being dyslexic.

Over the last 20 years or so, researchers have increasingly sought to investigate the nature of dyslexia across different languages. One useful comparison has been between dyslexic readers of German (which is transparent to read although rather opaque to spell) and English (which is opaque to read and spell). As German and English developed from the same Germanic root, they have many words in common; for example, the German words *Ball*, *Katze*, *Salat* and the English equivalents *ball*, *cat*, *salad*. The main difference in the pronunciation of these words lies in the vowels. While the 'a' in each of the German words is pronounced consistently as a short 'a' sound (as in the English word *cat*), the 'a' in each of the English words is pronounced inconsistently, as an 'aw' sound in *ball*, as a short 'a' sound in *cat*, and in the word *salad* as a short 'a' followed by an 'u' sound.

One study of 12 year old English and German children found that:

- English-speaking dyslexic children read their inconsistently-spelt, common English words (e.g. *young* and *mother*) with around 81 per cent accuracy; they read inconsistently-spelt, uncommon English words (e.g. *sword* and *comb*) with around 48 per cent accuracy; and made-up words (e.g. *hoat*, formed from the English words *hand* and *boat*) with around 27 per cent accuracy.

- German-speaking dyslexic children read their consistently-spelt, common German words (e.g. *jung* and *Mutter*) with around 97 per cent accuracy; they read uncommon German words (e.g. *Schwert* and *Kamm*) with around 89 per cent accuracy; and made-up words (e.g. *Hoot*, formed from the German words *Hand* and *Boot*) with around 77 per cent accuracy.

Due to the transparency of German, reading in Germany and Austria is taught mainly using phonics-based methods which stress the sounds of letters rather than their names. Children are encouraged to assemble words from their constituent sounds and they quickly learn which letters represent which sounds. This combination of the transparency of the language and an emphasis on phonics makes learning to read a relatively straightforward task for German-speaking children, even those with dyslexia, hence their almost perfect reading of real words (both common and uncommon), and their above 75 per cent accuracy for the reading of made-up words that they have never before encountered.

The English-speaking dyslexic children also read the common real words, which can be recognised by sight, with a reasonable degree of accuracy. However, their accuracy rates dropped below 50 per cent for the reading of uncommon words, and below 30 per cent for made-up words. Uncommon words are unlikely to be recognised by sight, and made-up words cannot be recognised as they have not been seen before, so these words need to be decoded according to the spelling-sound rules of the language. The opacity of English makes this decoding rather inaccurate for English-speaking dyslexic children.

While the consistency of German allows German-speaking dyslexic children and adults to develop fairly accurate reading skills, the difficulties of dyslexia manifest in these individuals (and in speakers of other transparent languages) in other ways such as slow reading speed. One early researcher found that when German dyslexic children read aloud a list of long words (of at least 11 letters each) they took between one-and-a-half and six times as long as non-dyslexic readers of the same age. For example, the word *Strassenbahnhaltestelle* (tram stop) took a non-dyslexic child on average 2-4 seconds to read, but a dyslexic child around 39 seconds. This same researcher documented one 11 year old dyslexic child's attempts at reading the word *Handarbeitslehrerin* (a female handicraft teacher):

- after 20 seconds the child attempted "Hander…"
- after 40 seconds, "Handbar…"
- after 60 seconds, "Handbarweisstellerin"
- and finally, after 90 seconds, "Handarbeitslehrerin"

More recently, other researchers have reported that 12 year old German dyslexic children read at the same speed as non-dyslexic readers who have the same reading age although these non-dyslexic readers are chronologically between four and six years younger than the dyslexic children.

The impairment in reading speed but not accuracy in speakers of transparent languages makes the recruitment of dyslexic participants for research studies rather problematic. For example, in one study involving English, French and Italian university students, the researchers had no difficulty identifying English and French dyslexic readers but to locate Italian dyslexic readers the researchers screened 1,200 adults on tests of spelling and stress assignment (while Italian spelling is transparent, some words are stressed in inconsistent and unpredictable ways when spoken). Those who scored in the bottom 10 per cent on these tests were tested further for speed of reading real words and made-up words, and on other tests of phonological ability which typically identify dyslexic readers of both transparent and opaque languages.

These tests included speed of naming written numbers, short-term memory for heard words, and the ability to swap over the initial sounds of two heard words such that *gold* and *silver* become *sold* and *gilver*. The students who scored in the bottom 10 per cent on these tests were identified as being dyslexic. The same tests were also given to the French and English dyslexic students and to non-dyslexic students from each country. The results showed that all three groups of dyslexic students performed more poorly than their non-dyslexic compatriots. Of particular note, however, while the Italian dyslexic readers were slower than the Italian non-dyslexic readers at reading real words, and particularly at reading made-up words, they were consistently more accurate than the English and French dyslexic readers on these tasks.

These, and similar, results suggest that German, English, French and Italian dyslexic readers – as well as dyslexic readers of many other languages – experience phonological difficulties although they manifest themselves in different ways depending on the transparency of the language. For example, around 97 per cent of first grade Greek non-dyslexic readers are able to read made-up words correctly, but this figure drops to 93 per cent for children with dyslexia. For Austrian children, figures of 96 per cent and 60 per cent are reported; for French children, these figures are 90 per cent and 75 per cent; and for Norwegian children, around 84 per cent and 74 per cent. Some researchers have found that for dyslexic readers of transparent languages these difficulties disappear within a few years by which time their phonological skills have 'caught up' with those of non-dyslexic readers.

As an example of this, German-speaking dyslexic readers from the third grade are almost perfect at spelling made-up words (they spell them in phonologically plausible ways) indicating that they have grasped the spelling-sound rules of their language. Similarly, while pre-school Dutch dyslexic children are poor at spotting which word out of three does not rhyme with the other two (demonstrating simple phonological difficulties), they are able to do this by the end of first grade. More difficult tests of phonological awareness, such as answering the question 'which word from *hat*, *cat*, *man*, *bat* ends in a different sound to the other three?' are beyond the capabilities of pre-school dyslexic children although they are able to perform these tasks as well as their non-dyslexic peers by the end of sixth grade. A combination of the transparent German and Dutch languages and phonics-based reading instruction enables dyslexic readers to overcome their early phonological difficulties, develop phonological awareness, learn letter-sound correspondences and become proficient readers.

A slightly different picture emerges from speakers of European Portuguese, which lies somewhere between English and German in terms of its transparency. While Portuguese is in some respects a fairly transparent language, some of its features actually make it rather opaque – for example, the fact that its five vowels may be pronounced in 18 different ways, and that in conversation many vowels are not pronounced, so written words cannot always be decoded letter by letter if they are to be read accurately. One study of fourth grade Portuguese dyslexic readers, fourth grade non-dyslexic readers (with the same chronological age as the dyslexic children), and second grade non-dyslexic readers (with the same reading age as the dyslexic children) tested their reading of regular words, made-up words and irregular words. This study found that:

- the dyslexic children read 92 per cent of regular words correctly, 82 per cent of made-up words, and 46 per cent of irregular words

- the older non-dyslexic children read 97 per cent of regular words correctly, 91 per cent of made-up words, and 83 per cent of irregular words

- the younger non-dyslexic children read 93 per cent of regular words correctly, 85 per cent of made-up words, and 68 per cent of irregular words.

All three groups were more accurate at reading regular words than made-up words or irregular words but over the three types of words, the dyslexic children's scores were more similar to those of the younger children matched for reading age than to those of the older children matched for chronological age. The authors interpreted this as indicating a developmental delay in the decoding abilities of the dyslexic children which they should overcome in time. They also note that as the dyslexic children were impaired relative to the older non-dyslexic children (which they would not be if they were reading a transparent language), then their reading is as would be expected of readers of an opaque language. However, the authors also point out that the dyslexic children were much worse at reading irregular words than either of the non-dyslexic groups which reflects a developmental deficit similar to that seen in dyslexic readers of other transparent languages. Therefore, the picture for these children is mixed, conforming neither wholly to that of dyslexic readers of transparent languages or opaque languages but somewhere in between.

Together, these findings show that phonological difficulties are a consistent feature of dyslexia across transparent and opaque alphabetic languages, at least through the early school years.

Dyslexia in non-alphabetic languages.

While the focus up to this point has been on alphabetic languages, this next section will look at dyslexia in two non-alphabetic languages: Chinese (Mandarin) and Japanese (Kanji and Kana).

People who do not speak Mandarin often think that it is an entirely pictographic language, i.e. that each of its spoken words is written as a single character. This is true of some of its characters but the majority (around 90 per cent) are compound characters made up of two elements which provide information about the meaning of the character and how to pronounce it. Mandarin is a tonal language, however. This means that words that would otherwise be pronounced in the same way are distinguished by their pitch which may be high, medium or low, rising, falling or constant. Therefore, the 408 syllables of Mandarin may be pronounced in approximately 1,300 ways with each pronunciation having its own meaning. For this reason Mandarin is considered to be an opaque language.

Although learning to read Mandarin requires less obvious phonological processing than that involved in learning to read alphabetic languages, phonological skills are still necessary, so the finding that Chinese dyslexic readers experience similar phonological difficulties to dyslexic readers of alphabetic languages is unsurprising. These phonological difficulties prevent Chinese dyslexic readers from benefiting from the phonological information provided by the phonetic elements of the printed characters.

Dyslexic readers tend to have difficulty analysing not only the sounds of words but also the written, visual forms. As most Mandarin characters are formed from around 9 to 11 individual strokes, dyslexic readers' visual difficulties are also likely to hinder their reading. The relative importance of visual and phonological skills has been explored in a study of dyslexic children in Hong Kong which found that relative to non-dyslexic readers of the same age:

- 29 per cent were less able to repeat words and non-words accurately, indicating phonological difficulties

- 42 per cent showed poorer knowledge of the structure of written characters, indicating visual difficulties

- 27 per cent showed poorer visual perception and visual memory
- 57 per cent were slower at naming written digits, indicating that they have difficulty mapping between written symbols and their spoken representations.

However, as this study failed to test younger children of the same reading age, we cannot know whether these difficulties are a cause or a consequence of the dyslexic children's reading difficulties. It may be that these children's poorer knowledge of the structure of written characters results from them spending less time reading than non-dyslexic children of the same age. Nevertheless, results from studies such as this one suggests that Chinese children with dyslexia have fundamental impairments in processing the sounds and visual forms of the language, just as dyslexic readers of alphabetic languages do.

A rather different picture emerges from the study of the written forms of Japanese – Kanji and Kana. Kanji is a pictographic script that was imported from China, and each character can be pronounced in two ways: one way according to the original Chinese word form, the other way according to the Japanese word form. Kanji characters provide no clue as to which of these pronunciations is correct in any sentence so this information is dictated by the context. By contrast, Kana is a phonetic script that has an almost perfect one to one relationship between its characters and the syllables in the spoken language.

Up until recently, dyslexia was relatively unknown in Japan so there were no accurate reports of its prevalence or manifestation. To investigate this, researchers tested almost

500 Japanese children in grades two to six on a battery of measures including the reading of Kanji and Kana characters and words. Children whose scores on the reading tests fell at the lower end of the distribution were identified as having reading difficulties. Accordingly, this study found that:

- 1.4 per cent of the children had difficulties reading the consistent Kana words; these children scored on average 95.5 per cent correct compared with the 99.5 per cent correct scored by the children without reading difficulties

- 6.9 per cent of the children had difficulties reading the inconsistent Kanji words; these children scored on average 81 per cent correct compared with the 95.5 per cent correct scored by the children without reading difficulties.

These results demonstrate that the reading of Kana is relatively straightforward for most children, even those identified as having reading difficulties. The reading of Kanji, with its inconsistent spelling-sound correspondences, is slightly more problematic for children with reading difficulties, but even so these children were able to achieve reading accuracy rates which far exceed those of dyslexic readers of English or Danish.

One interesting example which demonstrates the relative difficulties of reading English and Japanese is that of a 16 year old boy referred to in the literature as AS. This boy was born in Japan to an Australian father (a journalist and writer) and an English mother (an English teacher). He grew up in Japan to be completely bilingual – in the top 10 per cent of readers of his age in Japanese, but in English he was very dyslexic, displaying particular difficulty with reading, spelling and phonological processing. Clearly, AS's phonological difficulties existed whichever language he was reading, yet they only manifested themselves when he read a language (in this case English) that depends to a great extent on complex and irregular spelling-sound correspondences. The Japanese language presented few difficulties, and as such Japanese is considered by some to be an ideal language for dyslexic readers to learn.

Conclusion.

Phonological awareness is a good predictor of early reading development across languages but the role that phonological skills play in reading beyond the earliest stages depends on whether the language is transparent or opaque, alphabetic or non-alphabetic. The nature of the language also has a direct bearing on the manifestation of dyslexia: phonological difficulties cause relatively few problems for readers of languages with transparent letter-sound mapping, and dyslexic readers are identified primarily by their slow but accurate reading. By contrast, phonological difficulties can cause tremendous problems for readers of languages with opaque letter-sound mapping, and dyslexic readers are identified by their slow and inaccurate reading. Therefore, any research into dyslexia, and any interventions developed to support the reading of dyslexic children and adults, must take account of the relative consistency of the language if they are to be of any use whatsoever.

Chapter 2 – Phonological development across different languages[1].

Usha Goswami.

Introduction.

When babies are learning language, where do they begin? Theories of language acquisition used to assume that they began with the 'phoneme'. 'Phoneme' is a term used to refer to the individual sound elements that appear to make up words in languages. As literate adults, we hear these 'phonemes' very easily. We hear a spoken word like 'cat', and we hear three sound elements, that correspond to the 'sounds' made by the letters C, A and T. Classical linguistics assumed that all languages were based on two types of phoneme: consonant (C) phonemes and vowel (V) phonemes.

The elements used in a particular language were thought to be selected from a repertoire of around 600 consonants and 200 vowels that were distinctive to the human brain. Very recently, linguists have begun to revise these assumptions. For example Port (2007) commented it seems intuitively obvious that speech presents itself to our consciousness in the form of letter-like symbolic units. When we hear someone say 'tomato', we seem to hear it as a sequence of consonant and vowel sound units … [yet] there is virtually no evidence that supports the traditional view of linguistic representation. (Port, 2007: 143–4)

---

1   This article was originally published in The Routledge International Handbook of English, Language and Literacy Teaching (2010), edited by Dominic Wyse, Richard Andrews and James Hoffman, pages 98–109.

Port (2007) then systematically reviewed the linguistic evidence, assessing cherished assumptions, such as the existence of a 'universal phonetic inventory', whereby phonetic features from one language will overlap with those from another, since they are drawn from the same universal superset. He showed all these assumptions to be false. Where does such major theoretical revision leave babies who are learning to speak, and where does it leave literacy teachers who are helping children to learn to read?

The short answer is, that it doesn't matter for babies, but it matters rather a lot for teachers of literacy. This is because once we are literate ourselves, we can no longer perceive speech the way that a pre-literate child perceives speech. This makes it more challenging to teach literacy, as we are teaching children to hear sounds that we ourselves perceive to be fundamental to spoken words, but which are not in fact fundamental to spoken words. As Frith (1998) has pointed out, the acquisition of the alphabetic code is like catching a virus: 'This virus infects all speech processing, as now whole word sounds are automatically broken up into sound constituents. Language is never the same again' (p. 1051). There is growing evidence in the cognitive neuroscience literature that learning to read changes the brain, and growing understanding of how this occurs (see Goswami, 2008, for a simple review). In particular, there are experiments with adults showing that learning spelling patterns affects phonological (spoken language) judgements. For example adults are slower to decide that the spoken word 'sign' is a real word than they are for 'wine', because the spelling pattern '-ign' is less frequent, even though the spoken frequency of the words is similar (Ziegler *et al.*, 2004).

Although we as literate adults automatically hear spoken language as sequences of consonant and vowel sound units that are inextricably linked to overlearned letter sequences, children hear acoustically complex patterns that are linked to meanings. In learning letter-sound correspondences, children need to learn to pick out certain aspects of these complex representations, and ignore others. Many children can learn this easily, but others cannot. These individual differences in ease of learning are predicted by children's 'phonological awareness' skills. In this chapter, I will attempt an overview of our current understanding regarding these aspects of phonological development.

I will not, however, review the database for the theoretical claims made by Port (2007) and others, as it is quite large and beyond the scope of this chapter. Nevertheless, this database is important, and it is leading to radical revision of theoretical phonology and linguistics. The interested reader is referred to Pierrehumbert (2003); Port (2007) and; Vihman and Croft (2007). Here, I will consider the contributions of developmental phonology and of experimental studies of phonological development to the challenges facing literacy teachers of English.

The core aspects of phonological development.

Let us return to the question of where babies begin when they are learning spoken language. The new view in developmental phonology is that they learn language-specific 'phonotactic templates' (Vihman and Croft, 2007). A phonotactic template is essentially a phonological pattern. As such, it contains variations in sound intensity, pitch, duration and rhythm which together constitute a unit, usually of meaning. A common template for English is a bi-syllabic pattern with stronger fi rst syllable stress (a strong – weak stress template). The 'strong' fi rst syllable is typically louder, longer and higher in pitch than the second syllable. Familiar words that follow this pattern are 'Mummy', 'Daddy', 'biscuit' and 'baby'. This rhythmic pattern is so strong in English that we often change the words we use with babies and young children to conform to this pattern ('milkie', 'doggie'). Developmental phonologists like Vihman and Croft (2007) argue that babies' own babbling also conforms to these rhythmic patterns. Babies do not babble singlesyllable words. So both perception and production appear to converge onto these rhythmic templates.

The linguist Pierrehumbert (2003) calls these first acquisitions 'prosodic structures'. Importantly, however, typical prosodic structures or phonotactic templates vary across languages. In French, for example the dominant prosodic pattern is to lengthen the final syllable. Similarly, although all languages are rhythmic, languages conform to different rhythm 'types'. Whereas English is a stress-timed language, with its rhythm determined by the stressing of syllables that occur at roughly equal intervals in speech, French is a syllable-timed language, with its rhythm determined by stressing the last syllable in a particular word. Clearly, for non-native speakers of English, the phonotactic templates that organize a pre-literate child's phonological development may be rather different from the templates that govern phonological development in English. This will naturally have implications for learning to be literate in English.

Cross-language similarities.

Nevertheless, there are a number of important similarities in phonological organization across languages. For example when mothers and fathers talk to their babies, they talk in a particular way (called Motherese, or Infant-directed Speech). This way of talking emphasizes prosodic cues: pitch is typically heightened, duration is increased and rhythm and intonation are exaggerated. These features are found across the world's languages (Fernald *et al.*, 1989), and the use of infant-directed speech is universal because it appears to have a language-learning function, for example in word boundary segmentation (e.g. Echols, 1996). So the acoustic features that are important for phonology seem to be similar across languages. Another critical universal feature with respect to becoming literate is that the syllable is the primary perceptual unit in all languages.

Again, although most of the experimental data for this insight has come from adult work (e.g. Greenberg and Ainsworth, 2006), some of the data comes from experiments with young children. When young children are asked to reflect upon spoken language and perform 'phonological awareness' tasks, they do so most easily at the syllable level.

This can be illustrated by considering young children's performance in the different cognitive tasks that have been used across languages as measures of syllable awareness. Children can be asked to tap once with a stick for each syllable in a word (e.g. president = 3 taps), to put out a counter for each syllable in a word (e.g. telephone = 3 counters), or to make 'same–different' judgements about words (e.g. whether 'hammer' and 'hammock' share a syllable).

Children across languages generally show high levels of performance in tasks measuring their awareness of syllabic structure, from age 3–4 years (e.g. Liberman *et al.*, 1974; Cossu *et al.*, 1988; Treiman and Zukowski, 1991). For example in Treiman and Zukowski's same–different judgement task 100 per cent of fi ve-year-olds, 90 per cent of six-year-olds, and 100 per cent of seven-year-olds made accurate same–different judgments about syllables. Similar data have been reported for Turkish kindergartners (Durgunoglu and Oney, 1999), who tapped out 94 per cent of syllable structures correctly; Norwegian kindergartners, who counted out 83 per cent of syllable structures correctly (Hoien *et al.*, 1995); and German kindergarten children, who performed at 81 per cent correct in a syllable counting task (Wimmer, Landerl, Linortner & Hummer, 1991. These data show that when pre-reading children are asked to refl ect upon the phonological structure of spoken language at the syllable level, they can perform extremely well, across languages.

Cross-language differences.

Despite the ubiquity of the syllable as a perceptual linguistic unit across languages, structural elements of the syllable will vary across languages. Examples of factors that vary systematically include the number of sound elements within syllables (syllable complexity – a consonant-vowel (CV) syllable is 'simple', a CCVCC syllable is 'complex'); the types of sound elements within syllables ('sonority profi le'); and phonological 'neighborhood density' (the number of similar-sounding syllables to a particular target syllable in a given language). These factors will all affect the development of phonology and phonological awareness in young children.

Syllable complexity.

Taking syllable complexity first, it is striking that most world languages have syllables with a simple structure. To the literate brain, these languages comprise syllables with a consonant unit followed by a vowel unit. We might expect that it is easier to become 'phonologically aware' of the individual sound elements in syllables that have this simple CV structure. The English language has primarily complex syllables. The primary structure in English is CVC. For single syllable words (of which English has more than most languages), this structure accounts for 43 per cent of monosyllables (e.g. 'cat', 'dog', 'soap', 'look'; see De Cara and Goswami, 2002). English also has many CCVC syllables (15 per cent of monosyllables, e.g. 'trip', 'plan' and 'spin'); CVCC syllables (21 per cent of monosyllables, e.g. 'fast', 'pant' and 'jump'), and some CCVCC syllables (six per cent, e.g. 'crust').

Only five per cent of monosyllabic words follow the CV pattern ('sea', 'go', 'do'). It is perceptually challenging to segment a complex syllable like 'pant' into four distinct elements, which is why children often omit sounds like the penultimate consonant phoneme when they learn to spell (e.g. writing PAT for 'pant') (Treiman, 1998). Note also that the dominant phonological CVC template in English does not necessarily correspond to a CVC spelling – 'soap', 'look', and all 'magic E' words like 'cake' and 'time' follow a CVC phonological pattern. However, if a child spells these words using a CVC orthographic pattern (for example SOP, TIM) – this spelling is wrong. Children's 'invented spellings' are actually a rich source for understanding their phonological insights (see Read, 1986; Treiman, 1993; for systematic analyses).

Sonority profile.

The types of sound elements that comprise syllables also vary across languages. This variation is described by the linguistic term 'sonority profi le'. Vowels are the most sonorant sounds that we can make, followed in decreasing order by glides (e.g. /w/), liquids (e.g. /l/), nasals (e.g. /n/), and obstruents or plosive sounds (e.g. /p/, /d/, /t/). Linguists have debated whether there is an optimal sonority profi le, namely a profile that is frequently represented across languages because it is easy to produce (e.g. Clements, 1990). For example more sonorant sounds should be nearer to the vowel (we say 'tra' but not 'rta'). The majority of syllables in English end with obstruents (such as 'dog' and 'cat' – around 40 per cent). In contrast, the majority of syllables in French either end in liquids or have no coda at all (almost 50 per cent). To date, the effects of sonority profile with respect to the development of phonological awareness have not been investigated systematically across languages. Nevertheless, a priori it seems likely that sonority profile will have important effects on children's ability to segment syllables into smaller elements of sound (De Cara *et al.*, 2001).

Phonological neighbourhood density.

Phonological neighbourhood density is an interesting structural factor. It was originally proposed by psycholinguists working within the theoretical perspective of 'phonemic phonology' as a metric for describing similarities and differences between words in terms of shared phonemes (e.g. Landauer and Streeter, 1973; Luce and Pisoni, 1998).

However, when phonological neighbourhood density was analysed for spoken English, it turned out to highlight the perceptual salience of phonological similarity at the level of rhyme (De Cara and Goswami, 2002). In these analyses, phonological 'neighbours' are defined as words that sound similar to each other. The classical linguistic definition of a phonological neighbourhood is the set of words generated by the addition, deletion or substitution of one *phoneme* to the target (e.g. Landauer and Streeter, 1973; Luce and Pisoni, 1998). For example the neighbours of the target *ram* would include *ramp*, *am*, *rap* and *rim*. When many words resemble the target, the neighbourhood is said to be dense. When few words resemble the target, the neighbourhood is said to be sparse.

Neighbourhood density is highly correlated with another measure of syllable structure called *phonotactic probability* (Vitevitch *et al.*, 1999). Phonotactic probability is the frequency with which particular *sequences* of sound elements occur in words in the English language (Jusczyk, Luce & Charles-Luce, 1994). Words that have many phonological neighbours tend to be made up of sound elements that are frequent in occurrence.

Developmental psycholinguists quickly pointed out that if phonological neighbourhood density was to be used as a developmental metric, it was necessary to redefine the concept of a phonological 'neighbour'. Dollaghan (1994) reported that the onephoneme-different criterion of a phonological neighbourhood led to many intuitively dissatisfying exclusions when she attempted to calculate children's phonological neighbourhoods.

For example the one-phoneme different criterion excluded many rhyme neighbours, such as *clock* and *sock* (you cannot create *clock* by adding or substituting a single phoneme of *sock*). De Cara and Goswami (2002) provided empirical data that supported Dollaghan's view. They calculated phonological similarity neighbourhoods on the basis of the addition, substitution or deletion of a single onset, nucleus or coda.

The *onset* is a linguistic unit corresponding to any consonant phonemes before the vowel in a syllable (such as the 'cl' sound in *clock* and the 'str" sound in *string*). The *nucleus* is the linguistic term for the vowel, and the *coda* is a linguistic unit corresponding to any consonant phonemes after the vowel in a syllable, such as the /k/ sound in *clock* or the sound made by the letters 'mp' in *jump*. Linguists also use the term *rime* to refer to the unit comprising the nucleus and coda in any syllable.

While rime and rhyme are the same sound unit for monosyllabic words, they differ for bisyllabic words. Although 'mountain' rhymes with 'fountain', it does not rhyme with 'captain'. The individual rimes in each syllable in these words are the sound patterns made by the letter strings 'ount', 'ain' and 'ap'. The statistical analyses of De Cara and Goswami (2002) were carried out for all monosyllabic English words in the CELEX corpus (4,086 words; Baayen *et al.*, 1993), and for a number of smaller English lexica that were controlled for age of acquisition.

These statistical analyses showed that most phonological neighbours in English are rime neighbours (e.g. *clock*/ *sock*). This means that the phonology of English is rhyme-based, at least at the monosyllabic level. An example of a dense phonological neighbourhood in English is words that rhyme with *fair*. An example of a sparse phonological neighbourhood in English is words that rhyme with *moth*. In later work (Ziegler and Goswami, 2005), we carried out similar statistical analyses for German, French and Dutch. The German and Dutch analyses were based on the monosyllabic words in the CELEX database (Baayen *et al.*, 1993), and the French analyses were based on the monosyllabic words in BRULEX (Content *et al.*, 1990). The analyses showed that rime neighbours predominate in French, Dutch and German phonology as well. In all of these languages, the percentage of rime neighbours in the monosyllabic lexicon is between 40 per cent and 50 per cent.

Outstanding research questions.

Therefore, phonological neighbourhood density is a syllable-level factor that may be similar for some languages, and different for others. To date, to my knowledge, the effects of phonological neighbourhood density on the development of phonological awareness have only been examined for English. For English, words from dense phonological neighbourhoods are easier to identify in rhyme judgement tasks (De Cara and Goswami, 2003), and they are also easier to remember in short-term memory tasks (Thomson *et al.*, 2005). Storkel (2001) reported that young children who were taught nonword labels for unfamiliar objects were more likely to acquire labels from dense neighbourhoods, and Metsala (1999) reported that three- and four-year-old children could blend spoken phonemes to yield words from dense neighbourhoods more easily than to yield words from sparse neighbourhoods.

Hence this structural factor has an impact on children's phonological development for English. It seems important to examine the effects of this factor systematically across languages. When languages share phonological structure at this level (e.g. if rime neighbours are dominant in English and French), then theoretically this should facilitate cross-language transfer of phonological awareness. Certainly, cross-language comparisons show that young children are phonologically aware of onsets and rhymes before they become literate in all languages so far studied (see Ziegler and Goswami, 2005, for a comprehensive review).

This kind of information about phonological structure seems likely to be important for a systematic analysis of the acquisition of literacy in English by second language learners. Once we have systematic data showing the degree to which a child's native language is similar to English in terms of syllable complexity, syllable sonority profi le and phonological neighbourhood density, we may be able to predict the ease with which that child will become literate in English. For example sonority profi le is similar for English and German syllables, but different for English and French. Prosodic templates are similar in English and German, but different in English and French. Theoretically, the number of shared versus dissimilar factors would be expected to affect the cross language transfer of phonological awareness and the acquisition of literacy. However, these are empirical questions, and the data to answer them are not yet available. As well as yielding information important for predicting second language literacy acquisition, these linguistic factors may also affect second language spoken acquisition – at least, when the second language is acquired some time after birth.

Re-representing phonology as letters are learned.

Information about the phonological structure of a language by itself, however, will only provide a partial answer to whether second language learners might find it easier or more difficult to acquire literacy in English. This is because, as already noted, the way in which the brain represents phonology changes as reading skills are acquired. As Port (2007) commented, once we are literate 'speech [seems to present] itself to our consciousness in the form of letter-like symbolic units'. Hence the ease or difficulty with which the orthography of a language supports the development of these 'letter-like symbolic units' (classically, these units are called *phonemes*) will also play a role in literacy acquisition in different languages, and in the transfer of literacy skills between languages. This factor is called *orthographic consistency* or *orthographic transparency*.

Elsewhere, we have provided detailed analyses to demonstrate that the orthographic consistency of different European languages has profound effects on how rapidly children learning those languages develop an awareness of phonemes (Ziegler and Goswami, 2005). Similarly, we have shown how differences in orthographic consistency are systematically related to how rapidly children learning different languages become efficient at single word reading (Ziegler and Goswami, 2005, 2006). Essentially, we demonstrated that children acquiring reading in languages that have high orthographic consistency, or largely one-to-one mappings between letters and sounds, learn about phonemes more rapidly. In these languages, for example Finnish, Greek, German, Spanish and Italian, a letter corresponds consistently to one phoneme.

In contrast, languages like English, French, Portuguese and Danish have a one-tomany mapping between letters and phonemes. English has a particularly high level of orthographic inconsistency, as many letters or letter clusters can be pronounced in more than one way. Examples include O in 'go' and 'do', EA in 'bead' and 'bread', and G in 'magic' and 'bag' (see Berndt *et al.*, 1987; Ziegler *et al.*, 1997). Unsurprisingly, it is easier for a child to become aware of phonemes if one letter consistently maps to one and the same phoneme. Children learning to read languages like Finnish, Spanish and Italian acquire phoneme awareness relatively quickly. It is more difficult to learn about phonemes if a letter can be pronounced in multiple ways. Children learning to read languages like French and English acquire phoneme awareness more slowly (see Ziegler and Goswami, 2005, 2006, for more detailed evidence).

A table showing cross-language variation in the development of phoneme awareness, based on the phoneme counting task, is provided as Table 9.1. Similar differences between languages are found if grapheme–phoneme recoding to sound is the dependent variable (i.e. if children are asked to read aloud simple words and nonwords).

Seymour *et al.*, (2003) reported enormous differences in reading achievement during the first year of literacy instruction using measures of word and nonword reading (the word and nonword items used in their study were matched across languages). For example whereas Finnish children were reading 98 per cent of simple words accurately, English children (in Scotland) were reading only 34 per cent of matched items correctly. Whereas Italian children were reading 95 per cent of items correctly, French children were reading 79 per cent of items correctly. These data are also included in Table 9.1.

According to the theoretical analysis provided in this chapter, these cross-language differences in the development of phoneme awareness and simple reading skills are a product of *both* phonological factors and orthographic factors. Children learning to read in languages like Finnish, Italian and Spanish are not only learning orthographically consistent languages, but they speak languages with predominantly CV syllables. This means that onset-rime segmentation and phonemic segmentation are equivalent, as well as letters and sounds (phonemes) being (largely) equivalent. In contrast, children who are learning to read in languages like English are not only learning an orthographically inconsistent language, they also speak a language with predominantly complex syllables.

The cross-language comparisons noted in Table 9.1 are consistent with the proposal that it takes children longer to learn about phonemes and to become efficient in simple reading skills for languages like English and French compared to languages like Finnish, Italian and Spanish. However, another factor that is likely to be important for cross-language differences in phonological development is morphology (Goswami and Ziegler, 2006). Morphological changes are frequently signalled by phonological changes. As an example, in Turkish 'evim' means 'in my house' and 'evin' means 'in your house'. As this single phoneme change (/m/ to /n/) is critical for language comprehension, it is a priori likely that Turkish morphology affects how rapidly Turkish children become aware of phonemes (Durgunoglu, 2006). However, at the time of writing, the cross-language database on how morphological differences affect phonological development is too small to attempt a systematic analysis.

Conclusion.

In this chapter, I have discussed a number of the linguistic factors that affect the development of phonological representations of spoken language by children, and I have also sketched out the transformative effects on phonological development of becoming literate in an alphabetic language. I have suggested that these same factors will affect how easily non-native speakers of English (such as migrant children and other second language learners) can learn to be literate in English, as well as (perhaps) acquire English phonology.

Language	% phonemes counted correctly	% familiar real words read correctly[8]	% simple nonwords read correctly[8]
Greek	98[1]	98	97
Turkish	94[2]	-	-
Italian	97[3]	95	92
German	81[4]	98	98
Norwegian	83[5]	92	93
French	73[6]	79	88
English	70[7]	34	41

Table 9.1 Illustrative data (% correct) from studies comparing phoneme counting, simple word reading and nonword reading in different languages in Kindergarten or early Grade1.

Notes.

1 = Harris and Giannouli, 1999.

2 = Durgunoglu and Oney, 1999.

3 = Cossu *et al.*, 1988.

4 = Hoien *et al.*, 1995.

5 = Wimmer *et al.*, 1991.

6 = Demont and Gombert, 1996.

7 = Liberman *et al.*, 1974.

8 = Seymour *et al.*, 2003 (familiar real words = content and function words, nonwords = monosyllabic items only).

Prior to schooling, the research evidence suggests that phonological development is affected by factors like the prosodic templates that characterize the spoken syllables in a language, the phonological complexity of syllable structure in that language, the sonority profile of the syllable and the phonological neighbourhood density characteristics of the spoken phonology. Phonological development is also likely to be affected by the morphology of a language, with agglutinative languages like Finnish and Turkish possibly facilitating the development of phoneme awareness. As schooling begins, *orthographic consistency* exerts further effects on phonological development. These effects are profound: as noted already, 'language is never the same again' (Frith, 1998: 1051).

I have tried to show that psycholinguistics has come a long way in terms of recognizing which linguistic factors might be particularly worthy of study if we want a principled and systematic understanding of how to teach English literacy most effectively to second language learners. An overarching theoretical framework underpinning the discussion has been *psycholinguistic grain size theory* (Ziegler and Goswami, 2005, 2006).

This offers a unifying theoretical framework for understanding the kinds of internal phonological representations that the brain will develop in response to learning both spoken and written language. For example the theory predicts that for a child exposed to a consistent orthography, these phonological representations will differ from the kinds of internal representations that the brain will develop if the same child is exposed to an inconsistent orthography.

However, the effects of orthographic consistency and of the other factors discussed above can only be explored systematically if it is possible to devise language comparisons where all factors except one can be held constant. As languages vary naturally in many dimensions, this is diffi cult to achieve. Nevertheless, language pairings can be found that enable particular comparisons. For example English–German comparisons have been very fruitful, as English and German share phonological structure but differ in orthographic consistency. Studies exploring phonological development in these two languages suggest both system-wide effects of spelling consistency on phonological awareness, and item-specifi c effects (Goswami, Ziegler & Richardson, 2005).

Learning to read in all languages depends on phonological awareness, but cross-language variation in prosodic templates, syllable structure and orthographic consistency lead to cross-language divergence in the development of phonemic awareness and the achievement of alphabetic literacy. The implications for teaching are various.

For example within a particular language such as English, a better understanding of the importance for phonological development of factors like the complex syllable structure of spoken English, the importance of rhyme (via the neighbourhood density characteristics of English) and the stress-based prosodic system can help teachers to build a strong language foundation prior to literacy teaching that will facilitate the acquisition of alphabetic literacy.

When teachers must instead teach children for whom English is a second language, then an appreciation of the nature of the prosodic templates that characterize the spoken syllables in the child's first language, the phonological complexity of syllable structure in that language, the sonority profile of the syllable, and the phonological neighbourhood density characteristics of the spoken phonology, should all help to support teaching phonological awareness in English.

Finally, if the child for whom English is a second language is already literate or partly literate in their first language, then an appreciation of the nature of the orthography of that first language (e.g. whether it is highly orthographically consistent) will help to identify areas of overlap and divergence with respect to teaching alphabetic literacy.

References.

Baayen, R.H., Piepenbrock, R. and van Rijn, H. (1993). *The CELEX Lexical Database (CD-ROM)*. Philadelphia, PA: Linguistic Data Consortium, University of Pennsylvania.

Berndt, R.S., Reggia, J.A. and Mitchum, C.C. (1987). Empirically Derived Probabilities for Grapheme-to-Phoneme Correspondences in English. *Behavior Research Methods, Instruments, & Computers* 19: 1–9.

Clements, G.N. (1990). The Role of the Sonority Cycle in Core Syllabification. In J. Kingston and M. E. Beckman (Eds) *Papers in Laboratory Phonology 1: Between the grammar and physics of speech*. Cambridge: Cambridge University Press, pp. 283–33.

Content, A., Mousty, P. and Radeau, M. (1990). BRULEX: A computerized lexical data base for the French language/ BRULEX. Une base de donnees lexicales informatisee pour le francais ecrit et parle. *Annee Psychologique* 90(4): 551–66.

Cossu, G., Shankweiler, D., Liberman, I.Y., Katz, L.E. and Tola, G. (1988). Awareness of Phonological Segments and Reading Ability in Italian Children. *Applied Psycholinguistics* 9: 1–16.

De Cara, B. and Goswami, U. (2002). Statistical Analysis of Similarity Relations among Spoken Words: Evidence for the special status of rimes in English. *Behavioural Research Methods and Instrumentation* 34(3): 416–23.

De Cara, B. and Goswami, U. (2003). Phonological Neighbourhood Density: Effects in a rhyme awareness task in five-year-old children. *Journal of Child Language* 30: 695–710.

De Cara, B., Goswami, U. and Fayol, M. (2001). *Phonological Development and Spelling across Orthographies: Role of sonority and spelling-sound consistency*. Paper presented at the XIIth conference of the European Society for Cognitive Psychology, Edinburgh, September.

Demont, E. and Gombert, J.E. (1996). Phonological Awareness as a Predictor of Recoding Skills and Syntactic Awareness as a Predictor of Comprehension Skills. *British Journal of Educational Psychology* 66: 315–32.

Dollaghan, C.A. (1994). Children's Phonological Neighbourhoods: Half empty or half full? *Journal of Child Language* 257–71.

Durgunoglu, A.Y. (2006). Learning to Read in Turkish. *Developmental Science* 9: 437–8.

Durgunoglu, A.Y. and Oney, B. (1999). A Cross-linguistic Comparison of Phonological Awareness and Word Recognition. *Reading & Writing* 11: 281–99.

Echols, C.H. (1996). A Role for Stress in Early Speech Segmentation. In J. L. Morgan and K. Demuth (Eds) *Signal to Syntax: Bootstrapping from speech to grammar in early acquisition*. Mahwah, NJ: Lawrence Erlbaum Associates, pp. 151–70.

Fernald, A., Taeschner, T., Dunn, J., Papousek, M., Boysson-Bardies, B. and Fukui, I. (1989). A Cross-language Study of

Prosodic Modifications in Mothers' and Fathers' Speech to Preverbal Infants. *Journal of Child Language* 16: 477–501.

Frith, U. (1998). Editorial: Literally changing the brain. *Brain* 121: 1051–2.

Goswami, U. (2008). Reading, Dyslexia and the Brain. *Educational Research* 50(2): 135–48.

Goswami, U. and Ziegler, J.C. (2006). Fluency, Phonology and Morphology: A response to the commentaries on becoming literate in different languages. *Developmental Science* 9: 451–3.

Goswami, U., Ziegler, J. and Richardson, U. (2005). The Effects of Spelling Consistency on Phonological Awareness: A comparison of English and German. *Journal of Experimental Child Psychology* 92: 345–65.

Greenberg, S. and Ainsworth, W. (Eds) (2006). *Listening to Speech – An Auditory Perspective.* Hillsdale, NJ: Lawrence Erlbaum Associates.

Harris, M. and Giannouli, V. (1999). Learning to Read and Spell in Greek: The importance of letter knowledge and morphological awareness. In M. Harris and G. Hatano (Eds) *Learning to Read and Write: A cross-linguistic perspective.* Cambridge: Cambridge University Press, pp. 51–70.

Hoien, T., Lundberg, L., Stanovich, K.E. and Bjaalid, I.K. (1995). Components of Phonological Awareness. *Reading & Writing* 7: 171–88.

Jusczyk, P.W., Luce, P.A. and Charles-Luce, J. (1994). Infants' Sensitivity to Phontactic Patterns in the Native Language. *Journal of Memory and Language* 33: 630–45.

Landauer, T.K. and Streeter, L.A. (1973). Structural Differences between Common and Rare Words: Failure of equivalence assumptions for theories of word recognition. *Journal of Verbal Learning and Verbal Behaviour* 12: 119–31.

Liberman, I.Y., Shankweiler, D., Fischer, F.W. and Carter, B. (1974). Explicit Syllable and Phoneme Segmentation in the Young Child. *Journal of Experimental Child Psychology* 18: 201–12.

Luce, P.A. and Pisoni, D.B. (1998). Recognising Spoken Words: The neighbourhood activation model. *Ear & Hearing* 19: 1–36.

Metsala, J.L. (1999). Young Children's Phonological Awareness and Nonword Repetition as a Function of Vocabulary Development. *Journal of Educational Psychology* 91: 3–19.

Pierrehumbert, J. (2003). Phonetic Diversity, Statistical Learning and Acquisition of Phonology. *Language & Speech* 46: 115–54.

Port, R. (2007). How are Words Stored in Memory? Beyond phones and phonemes. *New Ideas in Psychology* 25: 143–70.

Read, C. (1986). *Children's Creative Spelling*. London: Routledge.

Seymour, P.H.K., Aro, M. and Erskine, J.M. (2003). Foundation Literacy Acquisition in European Orthographies. *British Journal of Psychology* 94: 143–74.

Storkel, H.L. (2001). Learning New Words: Phonotactic probability in language development. *Journal of Speech, Language & Hearing Research* 44: 1321–37.

Thomson, J., Richardson, U. and Goswami, U. (2005). Phonological Similarity Neighbourhoods and Children's Short-term Memory: Typical development and dyslexia. *Memory and Cognition* 33(7): 1210–19.

Treiman, R. (1993). *Beginning to Spell: A study of first-grade children*. New York: Oxford University Press.

Treiman, R. (1998). Beginning to Spell in English. In C. Hulme and R. M. Joshi (Eds) *Reading and Spelling: Development and disorders*. Mahwah, NJ: Lawrence Erlbaum Associates, pp. 371–93.

Treiman, R. and Zukowski, A. (1991). Levels of Phonological Awareness. In S. Brady and D. Shankweiler (Eds) *Phonological Processes in Literacy*. Hillsdale, NJ: Erlbaum.

Vihman, M. and Croft, W. (2007). Phonological Development: Towards a 'radical' templatic phonology. *Linguistics* 45: 683–725.

Vitevitch, M.S., Luce, P.A., Pisoni, D.B. and Auer, E.T. (1999). Phonotactics, Neighbourhood Activation and Lexical Access for Spoken Words. *Brain & Language* 68: 306–11.

Wimmer, H., Landerl, K., Linortner, R. and Hummer, P. (1991). The Relationship of Phonemic Awareness to Reading Acquisition: More consequence than precondition but still important. *Cognition*, 40: 219–49.

Ziegler, J.C. and Goswami, U. (2005). Reading Acquisition, Developmental Dyslexia and Skilled Reading across Languages: A psycholinguistic grain size theory. *Psychological Bulletin* 131(1): 3–29.

Ziegler, J.C. and Goswami, U. (2006). Becoming Literate in Different Languages: Similar problems, different solutions. *Developmental Science* 9: 429–53.

Ziegler, J.C., Ferrand, L. and Montant, M. (2004). Visual Phonology: The effects of orthographic consistency on different auditory word recognition tasks. *Memory & Cognition* 32: 732–41.

Ziegler, J.C., Stone, G.O. and Jacobs, A.M. (1997). What's the Pronunciation for -OUGH and the spelling for /u/? A database for computing feedforward and feedback inconsistency in English. *Behavior Research Methods, Instruments, & Computers* 29: 600–18.

Chapter 3 – Identifying Dyslexia of Learners with English as an Additional Language.

Kathleen Kelly and Sylvia Phillips.

Although we use the term 'English as an Additional Language' (EAL) in this chapter, this does not imply that learners with EAL can be considered as an homogeneous group. We use this term to describe learners whose first language or the first language used by their parents is not English. They include children and young people:

- born in another country who learned to speak another language and who may have come to England with no prior knowledge of English. There is a range of experiences here – some may have been in England for some time and acquired some English prior to starting at a primary school here, whereas others may only have arrived at a later stage of schooling. Even within this broad grouping, there is considerable diversity of first languages, experiences in home countries, culture and religion, and their experiences in England.

- who may have been born in the UK but have parents (or one parent) who speak no – or very little – English. Some may have siblings or other relatives who speak English to them, but some do not. They may well, therefore, not speak English at home.

- who are 'bilingual' at home, in that parents use both English and another language with them on a regular basis. However, they will not necessarily have achieved the same level of fluency or vocabulary in both.

- who are learning or using a first and second language other than English, so that English is not a 'second' language but a third or fourth, so that 'Additional Language' is a more appropriate term.

More than three hundred languages are now spoken in England and most schools have a population for whom English is **not** the first language and, therefore, can be described as 'multilingual'. These vary from schools where only two or three different languages can be found, to those where there are a hundred or more. As indicated above, however, there is a range of diversity in terms of learners' experiences of learning, speaking and using English.

A major concern for many teachers working in multilingual schools is to determine whether a learner with English as an Additional Language (EAL) has low achievement due to a learning difficulty or whether more time is needed to develop English language skills and adjust to the culture including the culture of school. Identification of a learning difficulty may be delayed because it may take some time to determine if a learner has a special educational need (as defined by the 1996 Education Act) or presents difficulties that commonly occur in acquiring an additional language. In recognition of the dilemma this poses, the SEN Code of Practice (DfES, 2001) emphasises the need to exercise 'particular care' and take into account the context of the 'home, culture and community' (paragraph 5:15) when identifying and assessing a special educational need. Whilst the Code points out that 'lack of competence in English must not be equated with learning difficulties', it does acknowledge that they **may** have learning difficulties (paragraph 5:16). This cautionary note is particularly relevant in the area of dyslexia where multilingual learners tend to be under-identified. Deponio *et al.,* (2000) found that very few teachers tended to consider dyslexia as a cause of the literacy difficulties of multilingual learners, suggesting that literacy difficulties may often inappropriately be attributed only to factors related to learning English as an additional language.

One of the ways of identifying dyslexia is to look for an uneven profile across subjects (e.g. performance in Maths or Science may be better than in English) or even within a subject, (e.g. learners may perform better orally than in written tasks). However, a spiky profile of a multilingual learner may reflect their developing English language skills. For example, Abdul who started school in England, aged seven, quickly acquired knowledge of the English number system and at age eight he performed well on tests of the four basic rules but was still struggling to construct sentences in written English and had a very limited English vocabulary.

Overlapping characteristics of dyslexia and early stages of development of EAL.

The difficulty of identifying dyslexia in multilingual learners in compounded by the fact that many of the indicators of dyslexia often occur as part of the normal acquisition of EAL in the early stages. Table 1 below shows characteristics that are often found on checklists for the identification of dyslexia together with examples of factors involved in early EAL acquisition that could offer a possible explanation:

Characteristics of dyslexia	Possible EAL factors
Reversals e.g. letters or words	Script of first language (L1) is right to left (e.g. Urdu) so learner sometimes reads right to left in English e.g. 'was' for 'saw'.
	Lack of familiarity with letter order e.g. 'hw' instead if 'wh'.
Omissions e.g. definite /indefinite article	Definite and indefinite articles do not exist in many Asian languages.
Omissions of parts of words	Endings could be missed due to L1 'interference' e.g. use of glottal stop in Chinese.
	Sound /letter may not exist in their L1
Vowel confusion	Lack of sensitivity to knowledge of English sounds.
	No written form of a short vowel (e.g. Arabic.)
Consonant confusion, e.g. voiced/unvoiced	Many Asian languages do not have voiced / unvoiced consonants. In Punjabi /p/ and /b/ are both voiced (and not distinguished by sound); In Gujerati /f/ and /v/ are both voiced.
	Thai has sounds 'half way' between /l/ and /r/ and half way between /k/ and /g/.
	No 'j' in Italian so confuse j/g.
Sequencing	Lack of familiarity with western culture e.g. mis-sequencing sets of pictures.
Sentence construction	Different grammatical order in L1
Very little written output	Lack of familiarity and confidence with English
	Differences in script between L1 and English e.g. L1 may be non-alphabetic
	L1 script may be logographic or printed
Naming difficulties	May substitute a word because of limited English vocabulary development
	No direct translation of the word inL1
	More choice of words in L1 than English which causes confusion
	Different cultural perspective e.g. labelled differently in L1
Slow processing speed /lack of automaticity	Not yet able to understand the language used
	May be translating into L1
Directionality e.g.	
Tracking difficulties in reading	L1 script goes right to left e.g. Urdu
Preposition confusion	No equivalent word in some languages

Table 1

It is important to note that the above table offers only examples from some different languages but it points to the significance of understanding as much as possible about the first language and culture of learners to appreciate the nature and possible reasons for the learning characteristics they present. Many of the characteristics listed above are involved in decoding (word recognition) and may offer an explanation as to why learners with EAL often put all their effort into decoding in the early stages at the expense of understanding the text. It is also clear from what is written above that using checklists such as those available from the British Dyslexia Association (which are extremely useful as a starting point for identifying dyslexia in learners where English is the first language) may lead to over-identification of dyslexia in learners in the early stages of English language acquisition.

What are the early stages of English language acquisition?.

We use the phrase 'early stages' to describe the acquisition of language that is needed for social situations and basic interpersonal communication. For example:

- Labelling objects or situations
- Following and giving instructions
- Asking and answering questions
- Describing objects, people, places or events
- Giving simple explanations or reasons

Cummins (1984; 2000) distinguished between this early stage of 'Basic Interpersonal Communication Skills' (BICS) and 'Cognitive and Academic Language Proficiency' (CALP).

He suggested that the BICS stage usually takes about two years to develop, although it is dependent on factors such as the languages of the home, and other experiences as discussed later. However, he pointed out that learners need to develop beyond this early stage in order to handle the cognitive and academic demands of education. These demands require learners to be able to:

- Follow and present arguments
- Make predictions
- Draw inferences
- Reach conclusions
- Offer explanations and alternative views
- Justify decisions or give a rationale
- Clarify thoughts
- Hypothesise
- Have an extensive vocabulary
- Be familiar with literary language including subject specific

This level of language proficiency may be needed in order to identify and assess learners for dyslexia and takes several more years to acquire.

Assessment for Dyslexia.

The majority of tests used in the UK have been developed and standardised on populations that are mainly English speaking and / or based on Western cultures. In the case of tests where learners with EAL have been included in the standardization sample, there is seldom any detail of the level of their English language skills.

In most cases, a good level of English proficiency is needed to access such tests. Research by Kelly (2002) of a class of 8-9 year old Pakistani children found low scores on several of the subtests of the Dyslexia Screening Test. An earlier study of Bengali children with five years exposure to English produced below average scores for all the children on a digit span test (see Kelly, 1993) suggesting that the norms were inappropriate.

These studies suggest that 4-5 years exposure to English may not be sufficient to develop the English proficiency needed for standardized tests that use norms that have been developed for a different population.

A formal assessment of dyslexia normally includes assessment of attainment in literacy (reading, spelling, writing), underlying reasoning ability (verbal and non-verbal) and either a screening test or diagnostic tests of working memory, phonological processing, and speed of processing.

Cultural and linguistic bias is usually easily identified in the format and content of verbal tests where demands are made on language proficiency and vocabulary. Such tests may require a learner to explain the meaning of a word (expressive vocabulary as in the Mill Hill Vocabulary Test) or to demonstrate the understanding of a given word by pointing to an appropriate picture (receptive language, as in the British Picture Vocabulary Scale 3).

These tests, like those of reading and listening comprehension, clearly require a certain level of language proficiency and exposure to a range of experiences to acquire relevant vocabulary and information.

It is also the case, however, that many tests used in the formal assessment of learning difficulties in general (including dyslexia) are tests of cognitive abilities. Among these are tests of 'learning ability' sometimes known as 'intelligence' tests. These can include both a verbal and non-verbal element and have often been used as 'aptitude tests' to point to the ability to learn and adapt to the environment, largely based on how one reasons or approaches 'new' or unfamiliar tasks.

Whilst verbal tests reflect what one has already learned (and could therefore be compared to 'achievement' tests), 'non-verbal' tests were, for a long time, considered to be better measures of assessing more abstract reasoning, 'free' from linguistic and cultural bias. Such tests pose problems in pictorial or diagrammatic forms which are 'unfamiliar' to the learner being assessed.

Examples of such tests are matrices tests (as in the Wide Range Intelligence Tests (WRIT) and Raven's Progressive Matrices) where a logical series of patterns is presented and the learner has to work out the relationships involved in order to select the 'correct' final piece of the pattern from a choice of possible alternatives. A further example of non-verbal reasoning may be found in the 'Diamonds' test of the WRIT and in the Wechsler Intelligence Scale for Children (WISC-IVR).

Both tests include interpreting two-dimensional diagrams using three-dimensional materials. (n.b. WISC-IVR is used by educational psychologists whereas both WRIT and Raven's Progressive Matrices can be used by qualified specialist teachers.)

These 'non-verbal' tests were seen as better indicators of learning ability because they involved 'reasoning' (the ability to see relationships and produce similar relationships) without the need to use English / or even words. They are now only used in this way with great caution and are normally used to indicate visual and spatial perceptual skills rather than make assumptions about 'learning ability'. Ability to function appropriately in these tests, however, is also influenced by prior cultural experiences.

Early work by anthropologists and psychologists working in very different cultures (particularly different parts of Africa) found that not only was classification and categorisation of objects different depending on culture (regardless of language) but also responses to abstract patterns and ability to 'see' relationships in 'sets' of patterns differed and such non-verbal tests were certainly neither culture-free nor culture-fair. A particular focus for discussion was that children brought up in a 'carpentered-world', familiar with geometric patterns, straight lines etc. were advantaged in non-verbal tests.

For a discussion and overview of this area, see Montello (1995) and Davies (2007). The importance of experiences may suggest why children in England who have done jigsaw puzzles from an early age may, **at first**, have an advantage over those who have not, when undertaking 'matrices' tests. Naseem, a ten-year-old girl who speaks Punjabi and Urdu at home, enjoyed doing the Matrices test in WRIT saying, "It is like some of the brain-training games my Dad bought for me to use on the computer", suggesting that familiarity with the types of items may lead to a positive approach to the test situation.

Nevertheless, some non-verbal tests still make the claim that they measure 'g' or general underlying cognitive ability (see the manuals for Raven's Progressive Matrices (2010) and WRIT 2000). WRIT also distinguishes between 'fluid' (non-verbal which was claimed to be less influenced by experiences) and 'crystallised' (verbal ability which clearly reflects experience) intelligence. As indicated above, these claims are open to criticism. However, when we use such tests in the assessment of dyslexia we should be looking at the profiles they provide in relation to vocabulary knowledge and spatial / visual skills rather than using them as 'global' measures of ability. (This is the case for **all** learners not just those with EAL. It is particularly important, however, to bear in mind the implications of such assessment for learners from any ethnic minority groups including those with EAL.) The information should be used to target areas for intervention.

In the USA, since 2004, all tests must be conducted in a child's native language, where this is available. This is not the legal position in England currently and in any case, few tests are yet available in relevant languages. It is not appropriate merely to translate a test into English, as this does not overcome cultural bias in the understanding required. However, it is apparent that seeking a range of relevant standardisation populations is vitally important as the linguistic cultural and immediate community and educational experiences are so diverse that to attempt to develop any single form of assessment for learners with EAL may not be possible.

How can we identify dyslexia in learners with EAL?

It is clear from the above that there are some problems in identifying dyslexia when so many literacy difficulties may be related to acquiring the English language. However, it is important to retain the principle of the need for early identification of literacy difficulties. As with any learner, the use of dynamic assessment is useful. This will take account of how the learner approaches particular tasks and how they respond to any specific form of teaching and intervention.

The concept of 'Response to Intervention' (RTI) used widely in the USA as part of the assessment process for identifying learners who may need special educational provision (Pierangelo and Giuliani, 2009) is useful here. It may be that the teaching (grouping and / or curriculum content) has itself given rise to difficulties for a learner. Using and evaluating more appropriate methods **may** make a difference and / or point to underlying difficulties.

It is important to discover as much as possible about a learner's use of English and other languages outside school as well as considering what steps the school is taking to ensure that English language structures and vocabulary are being taught to support and develop proficiency in English. At the same time, it is important to show how a learner's home language and culture are valued in the school. Many schools do so through the books, stories, art and music they employ for all learners throughout the curriculum. It may be, however, that they do not know much about the nature and structure of a learner's 'first' language.

Some languages may use an alphabetic or logographic system; some may have a more 'transparent' orthography that English (i.e. the letter-sound (grapheme-phoneme) relationship may be much more regular, as in Spanish and Greek). In addition, a learner's lack of proficiency / fluency in both their spoken language and literacy in L1 is important. Does the learner have 'preferred' language – and why? Sometimes interpreters may be useful to find out about these aspects.

Although cognitive processing tests such as phonological awareness, working memory and rapid naming may appear more linguistically appropriate than literacy or vocabulary tests, there can be particular difficulties. As seen above, the phonological structures and systems vary in different languages, giving rise to what 'appear' to be difficulties but may be related to L1. We have also observed that many learners with EAL develop good skills in repeating and blending syllables spoken by an assessor even when these form 'nonsense' words.

This skill may suggest that they have 'learned' English by sounds rather than meanings! Working memory tests using recall of numbers and letters has not always seemed appropriate (Kelly, 1993). It may even be worthwhile to compare speed for rapid naming when speaking L1 and when using English to note whether there are any differences. Rapid naming tests using letters and numbers may prove a useful tool. However, any 'timed' test requires good preparation and understanding of the 'need' for speed. A further major issue with any timed test is that learners may 'translate' into a preferred language and then back again.

We have noted this particularly in tests of rapid naming of colours and objects, but less frequently in naming letters and numbers. This possibly reflects greater confidence in

English with numbers / letters because they are in regular use in the classroom. Developing rapid naming tests in L1 might be a promising step in assessing dyslexia.

If a learner appears to be having great difficulty in learning to read (and spell) despite having acquired some basic spoken English, then it may be useful to consider him or her to be 'at risk' of having dyslexia. This means that certain areas should be investigated, summarised below.

What should we take into account? Although we have found that many learners with EAL show very low levels of literacy **as a group** unless they have had 4-5 years learning English, it is not appropriate to wait this 'length of time before assessing for dyslexia. Length of time is only one factor. A ten-year old child who spoke Turkish until, coming to England at the age of nine, scored very well on tests of reading and spelling (in English) after only 10 months in an English school. Her English vocabulary (using BPVS) was, however, still very weak, and gave her an age-equivalent score of 3.5 although she could maintain a good conversation about her family and school.

We need to consider as much information as we can and suggest the following:

- Length of time being **taught** EAL, rate of progress made and level of proficiency
- Length of time being taught in an English school (in England) and general progress made
- Any formal test level known for EAL
- What language(s) are spoken in the home?

- What language(s) is / are spoken to the child?

- Do siblings use English to speak to each other?

- Do peers / friends in the neighbourhood speak English to this learner?

- What sort of experiences does the learner have out of school? (e.g. attending the mosque, visiting other cities, but maybe only to visit relatives). What language is used? It is interesting, for example, to compare Naseem's experiences with those of Jan, a boy of the same age, whose first language is Czech. At home, only Czech is spoken. There is a television (in many homes this is often a source of listening to English / widening learning experiences through English), but only Czech television is watched in Jan's house. He meets other members of his family and community, but, again, only Czech is spoken.

- What support does the learner get for developing / extending their use of English in school?

- Is there any specific targeting of developing vocabulary / sentence structure / knowledge of language functions going on in the school?

- How does this learner's use of English compare with:

- Peers with EAL in the same school?

- Peers who are native speakers of English?

Where a learner appears to be very slow to develop and use spoken English, then their level of proficiency in L1 should be taken into account. If a child also appears to be developing spoken L1 slowly, then the possibility of a general language / speech difficulty should be investigated by carrying out an assessment in L1. Where a learner's spoken English is developing normally but they have difficulties in decoding in English then their literacy level in L1 should be considered (if the child has learned to read in L1). Experiencing literacy difficulties in L1 may indicate underlying dyslexic-type difficulties.

As for any learner having difficulties resembling dyslexic-type difficulties, key questions are:

- What teaching / intervention (appropriate to these difficulties) has taken place and for how long?

- What has been the learner's response and rate of progress?

However, we believe that the most useful way forward, rather than seeking a formal 'label' at this early stage, is to offer appropriate support. This should include:

- Further development of EAL tuition by targeting the use of structured language and vocabulary development grounded in experiences

- Demonstrating the L1 is valued

- Cumulative, multi-sensory teaching which is phonics-based but which incorporates a morphological approach **and,** importantly, emphasises reading for meaning (comprehension) from early stages. Teaching will include developing memory (auditory and visual) and speed of processing / automaticity (as in many specialist programmes for learners with dyslexia e.g. Kelly and Phillips, (2011)

- Development of use of reading for enjoyment and information: familiarity with 'literary' language and comprehension e.g. through paired / shared reading.

There can be no doubt of the complexity of issues involved in diagnosing dyslexia in children with EAL. It is difficult to determine whether 'dyslexic' difficulties outweigh the influence of linguistic and cultural factors on any assessment procedures. At the time of writing the findings of recent research into dyslexia and multilingualism in primary schools (Mortimore, et al, 2011) have not yet been published, but a very interesting aspect of that research has been an emphasis on intervention. What is important is to meet the language and literacy needs of learners with EAL so that they can achieve educationally.

References.

Cummins, J. (1984) Bilingualism and Special Education: Issues in Assessment and Pedagogy, Clevedon: Multilingual Matters.

Cummins, J.(2000) Language, Power and Pedagogy: Bilingual Children in the Crossfire. Clevedon: Multilingual Matters

Davies, W.M (2007) Cognitive contours – recent work on cross-cultural psychology and its relevance for education in *Studies in Philosophy of Education*, 26, 13-42.

Deponio, P., Landon, J., Mullin, K. and Reid, G. (2000) An audit of the processes involved in identifying and assessing bilingual learners suspected of being dyslexic: a Scottish study, *Dyslexia*, 6 (1) 29-41.

Kelly, K. (2002) The early detection of dyslexia in bilingual pupils. Unpublished M. Ed. Thesis, Manchester Metropolitan University.

Kelly, K. and Phillips, S. (2011) Teaching Literacy to Pupils with Dyslexia: a multi-sensory approach. London: Sage.

Montello, D. (1995) How significant are cultural differences in spatial cognition? *Lecture Notes on Computer Science*, 988, 485-500

Mortimore, T., Northcote, A. and Hansen, L. (2011) *Dyslexia and Multilingualism.* Paper presented at BDA International Conference, Harrogate.

Pierangelo, R. and Giuliani, G.A. (2009) *Assessment in Special Education, 3rd Edition.* Upper Saddle River, N.J.: Pearson Education.

Chapter 4 – Identifying and supporting literacy acquisition in bilingual learners potentially at risk of dyslexia: The Big Lottery Dyslexia and Multilingualism Project.

Tilly Mortimore, Mim Hutchings and Anny Northcote.

Introduction.

The number of pupils in schools in Wales and England acquiring English as an additional language between 2008 to 2011 is rising year on year. Between 2008 and 2011 numbers rose from 14.4% to 16.8% in primary and 10.8% to 12.3% in secondary schools, involving an increase from 240 languages to over 300 by 2011 (NALDIC, 2011). Linguistic communities vary across schools, within an education system centred in the literacy system of English with few bilingual educational programmes; minority first language children are expected to learn to read and write fluently in this majority language.

Whilst most bilingual children are successful in their academic achievement, Ofsted had identified in 2003 underachievement of Black and Minority Ethnic students as a cause for concern. Issues emerge around teaching linguistically diverse children in the classroom in ways which support their bilingualism, alongside political dimensions to how bilingual learners are perceived and catered for in schools.

Social and cultural differences, life experiences and political policy, play a significant role in the development of EAL and literacy, indicating the need for a holistic approach, particularly when considering what to do when there is cause for concern in literacy skills or at stages such as Key Stage 2 when the demands upon reading comprehension, spelling and writing skills accelerate. The challenges encountered by children at risk of dyslexia at this stage are linked with difficulties with the rule systems of the second language, coping with the new phonology and orthography involved and making the transition from conversational language (Basic Interpersonal Communication Skills, BICS, Cummins, 2000) to the academic language increasingly required across the curriculum.

Whilst from 4 to 10% of all children may be predisposed to SpLD/dyslexia (Singleton, 2009), bilingual learners with English as a second language are under-represented in SpLD/dyslexia programmes and constitute a potentially overlooked vulnerable group. SpLD/dyslexia is hard to identify in children acquiring EAL with a high risk either of misattribution of a learner's difficulties to second language acquisition or misrecognition in schools of a child's underlying abilities, resulting in inappropriate application of SEN labels and expectations (Hall *et al.*, 2001).

Difficulties with acquiring a second language can mask signs indicating risk of SpLD/dyslexia and Snowling has highlighted the role played by levels of skill in oral language in the development or prevention of SpLD/ dyslexia (Snowling, 2010). Research (Ganschow and Sparks, 2000) confirms that strengths and weaknesses in the linguistic codes of phonology/orthography (sounds/letter patterns), syntax and semantics are transferred between languages, to the extent that learning a second language will challenge learners at risk of dyslexia because it also requires those skills frequently compromised in dyslexia – sequencing ability, phonological knowledge and both short- and long-term memory (Wolf, 2008). Listening difficulties can also arise from the processing differences associated with SpLD/dyslexia (Crombie & McColl, 2001) making a second language, as complex and inconsistent as English, challenging for dyslexic children to acquire (Crombie, 1997: Ziegler & Goswami, 2005).

There has been little research exploring the impact of interventions for this group. The most beneficial strategy for dyslexic learners is direct, systematic, multisensory instruction (Moats & Farrell, 2005; Brooks, 2002). This would apply also to the rule systems of a second language (Sparks & Miller, 2000). This type of teaching is the predominant mode of support for dyslexic learners and this mixed-methodology project aimed to fill a gap in the research and link the expertise resident in the separate domains of dyslexia and bilingual education.

The bilingual context – linguistic and cultural diversity.

Being bilingual refers to having access to and using two or more languages on a daily basis, (Baker 2006, Martin 2009). However a 'bilingual' speaker may not necessarily be competent and fluent in at least two languages across a range of oral and literate contexts. It is more likely that children in UK schools may operate at varying levels in two or more language domains. The closer the child is to full competence in two languages, the more likely this is to confer cognitive advantages (Baker, 2006).

Bilingualism is termed 'simultaneous' when children learn two languages from birth, usually the languages of parents and community. 'Consecutive' or 'sequential' bilingualism, common in the UK and for the project children, refers to those who learn a second language on entering social contexts, such as education or work (Baker 2006). Research suggests that a number of factors will affect a child's individual acquisition of spoken and written language. These will include previous educational practices, motivation, linguistic and cultural backgrounds, opportunities and support from home and school.

Furthermore, the extent to which the classroom acknowledges the cultural identity and gives high status to language 1 (L1) alongside the additional language, English, will enhance bilingual proficiency resulting in an 'additive bilingualism' with cognitive and social advantages. Many English schools, however, exhibit a more 'subtractive' context – when L2 takes precedence over L1, which can be seen as unimportant or a hindrance to learning the second language with consequently reduced self-esteem and loss of L1, potentially resulting in lower cognitive development and poorer achievement in English.

A child's culture influences every aspect of cognitive skills and aptitudes (Rogoff, 2003). Hence, individual children's stories, backgrounds, social and emotional development and previous educational experiences alongside their culturally diverse, multi-lingual communities must be acknowledged in any explanation of literacy acquisition (Cummins 2000) accepting that many difficulties may arise from school and teaching approaches rather than from within the children or from their attempts to acquire literacy in English.

Cross-linguistic literacy acquisition and dyslexic differences.

Socio-cultural differences, different ways of communicating and forms of language promote different cognitive skills (Rogoff, 2003). There is some evidence that acquiring literacy in L1 could benefit fluency and phonological awareness in L2, particularly if literacy instruction starts early (Bialystok, 2001). Knowledge about language is greater when more than one language is known. Metalinguistic awareness plays a role in bilingual children's ability to generalise through applying linguistic understanding across languages (Durgunoglu *et al.*, 1993).

Bilingual leaners do not have to relearn the language structure when acquiring a new language as they already know how language works. It has also been argued, however, that bilingual children, relatively new to English and still developing communicative skills, may have difficulties with some aspects of linguistic comprehension (Hutchinson *et al.*, 2003) when learning to read in L2. This can be exacerbated by multiple meanings within the text and the need for inferential reading. Hutchinson and colleagues attributed underachievement in L2 literacy to low levels of language fluency, particularly related to vocabulary and comprehension.

Researchers are, therefore, not totally in agreement over the enhancing effect of bilingualism (Lipka and Siegel, 2007) and although acquiring literacy in a simpler more regular or transparent orthography may confer an advantage when it comes to learning the complex and opaque orthography of English (Geva & Verhoeven, 2001), it is equally acknowledged that any weaknesses in L1 will transfer across to L2. Difficulties in both phonology and orthography, experienced in first language, will impact upon second language learning (Ziegler & Goswami , 2005).

Deficits in phonological processing, Rapid naming (RAN) and verbal short term memory (digit span, word span and non-word span) all predict reading skills across all orthographies, producing similar development in spelling and reading profiles in the first language (L1) and second language (L2) in spite of differing levels of proficiency in both. When learning the opaque English system, learners do need to develop their phonological processing skills and to be able to generalise across to new or infrequent words. Although experience of a more transparent orthography may have helped to reinforce phonological skills, the demands of English may prove too complex.

Wolf states,

> Reading in any language rearranges the length and breadth of the brain…. there are multiple pathways to fluent comprehension, with a continuum of efficiency taking varied forms among the varied writing systems. (2008, p. 64)

Different orthographies give rise to subtle differences in cognitive skills. The following factors are crucial to the understanding of a learner's proficiency in literacy in L2: the orthography, complexity and level of transparency of the learner's first language, plus the learner's oral proficiency in L1 and L2. Rose's (2009) identification of the main characteristics of dyslexia as difficulties in phonological processing, verbal memory and verbal processing speed is largely reinforced by cross-linguistic studies.

Will these be triggers across all languages? The focus and structure of the language will affect the difficulties identified (Wolf, 2008) so learners of a transparent language may struggle to become fluent, phonological problems will occur in opaque languages, while visuo-spatial memory issues arise with non-alphabetic scripts. Although the 'standard' phonological deficit remains a marker, it may not be so easy to spot in a bilingual child who is already literate in a transparent L1.

Possibly the phonological processing skills, so closely involved in the development of reading and spelling, may be enhanced both by acquiring some literacy in a transparent L1 and by the learning of a second language. In this case, those bilingual learners who still exhibit poor phonological skills may well be those at risk of dyslexia. The role of verbal processing speed is also evident and research (e.g. Wolf, 2008) indicates that poor fluency may be a stronger indicator of dyslexia in some languages than phonological processing difficulties.

The Dyslexia and Multilingualism Project.

This project has been ground breaking in several ways. It has combined expertise from two professional worlds, that of SpLD/dyslexia support and of those experts who support bilingual learners, to enable exchange of expertise. It has located bilingual learners in both rural and urban schools covering the full range of Social and Economic status (SES), including children who speak between them 43 languages. It has used a mixed methodology design to identify both the quantifiable impact of an intervention upon literacy scores and to explore the experiences of the Teaching Assistants (TAs) who delivered the intervention alongside the stories of some of the bilingual children and their parents.

The project aimed:

- to establish reliable ways of identifying EAL children who experience dyslexic type difficulties;
- to develop and trial appropriate strategies and materials for supporting these children;
- to provide training for SENCos and TAs involved in the project.

Identifying risk of dyslexia in bilingual children.

215 children from years 4-6 in 55 schools with higher than average numbers of bilingual learners from Liverpool, Manchester/Salford, Swindon, Bristol, Bath & South West and London embarked upon the project. They had all been in UK schools for a minimum of two years and had been selected as potentially at risk of dyslexia from 465 children, whose literacy was not developing as expected, using a combination of Lucid LASS Junior (8 – 11) Lucid Ability (Verbal Reasoning test only), the Dyslexia checklist adapted from Wesford (Ball, 2007) and the Working Memory Rating Scale (Alloway et al., 2008).

Later, the accuracy of results from the screening was explored by undertaking full individual dyslexia assessments with 45 pupils. Statistical analyses showed no significant links between the full assessment outcomes and the 'at risk of dyslexia' scores obtained from the LUCID/ LASS screeners. Dyslexia or Working Memory checklists, indicating that the sample of children in the project is not a group of children purely with dyslexia and also advising caution in the use of screeners as a 'diagnostic' tool.

However, questions also remain unanswered about the reliability of a full assessment in English rather than the learner's L1 and the need to explore the learner's context and story. The conclusion from this aspect of the project, and from comments from the SENCos , would be that information from these screeners is useful in compiling a profile to enable appropriate support to be designed but should be not be used as an indicator of dyslexia in bilingual learners at this age group.

Evaluating interventions for bilingual children.

Few studies had previously evaluated the efficacy of interventions for bilingual learners with dyslexia so the intervention programme, which aimed to take into account the learner's cultural background and experiences, was based upon needs identified in monolingual children with dyslexia (e.g. Brooks, 2002; Ott, 2007) and in dyslexic learners acquiring a modern second language (e.g. Schneider, 2009). It was, therefore, structured, reinforced, cumulative and multi-sensory, and incorporated a combination of strategies designed to improve phonological processing skills (including verbal memory), oral language development and explicit vocabulary teaching, explicit strategies to develop comprehension skills (such as reciprocal reading) work with morphemes and strategies to improve memory and processing speed.

Two computer delivered programmes designed to be dyslexia-friendly were adopted:

- *Nessy* (Net Educational Systems Ltd): games and activities to develop phonological awareness, word patterns and spelling rules;

- *Rapid Reading* (Pearson Heinemann), a reading scheme for KS2 which encourages discussion of ideas and vocabulary in the text and also includes speech recognition software for independent listening and reading practice.

Prior to the project, 76 SENCos, 106 TAs and 70 class teachers received two days of training in dyslexia, in working with bilingual learners, in assessment instruments and the intervention materials and the schools were issued with the screening materials and pre and post intervention assessment instruments – WRAT 4, BPVS, Non-word test (Turner, 1994) and YARC. A pair of children was allocated to each TA and the half hour intervention took place daily over a period of 15 weeks (maximum 75 sessions).

The intervention took place over two phases. The children's literacy skills were tested three times – pre Phase one, post phase one and at the end of Phase 2. Table A indicates the structure of the intervention.

	Group 1 N=101 students	Group 2 N=*** students	Group 3 N=*** students
Pre-testing Sept 2010	√	√	√
Phase 1: 15 weeks between Oct and March	NESSY/RR Intervention (A)	Paired reading (PR) (B)	Control – no intervention (C)
InterimTesting Feb/March 2011	√	√	√
Phase 2: 15 weeks Feb/March to July	No intervention	NESSY/RR (A)	NESSY/RR (A)
Final Testing July 2011	√	√	√

Table A: Structure of the project interventions.

To enable the impact of the specific NESSY/RR intervention to be explored, the children were divided into three groups, pairs who undertook the intervention, pairs who undertook a paired reading activity with a trained TA and a third waiting control group who had no individual support. Phase 2 enabled all the children to undertake the NESSY/RR intervention and established the extent to which any changes were sustained over time.

Table B shows the tests that were selected to measure the children's progress over the two phases of the project:

Attainment	Skills tested	Test	Tester
Reading	1. Accuracy; rate; comprehension	YARC	SENco
	2. Single word	WRAT4	SENco
	3. Silent reading	WRAT4	Senco
Spelling	Single word	WRAT4	SENco
Phonological decoding	Non-word decoding	Turner and Ridsdale (date)	SENco
Receptive language		BPVS	SENCo
Writing	**Free writing:** Story of your day : Word count: words per minute: length of time to complete in seconds % indecipherable Analysis based on National Curriculum SATS scales		TA in session Standard determined by 2 raters

Table B:

The Findings.

Phase One:

Practical considerations had meant that the children were not divided into the three groups randomly, as intended, and the control group's pre-test scores emerged as significantly stronger than those of the other two groups. Comparisons of pre and post phase one scores indicated that all three groups had made significant progress in all the skills tested with the exception of the control group's progress in single word reading, National Curriculum level (NC), number of words and legibility and speed of writing and the other two groups' progress in speed of writing.

However, when effect size of the changes were calculated, this indicated that both intervention groups outperformed the controls across all areas. In areas such as spelling, phonological decoding and reading accuracy, the children who had worked with NESSY and Rapid Reading performed better than the paired reading children. However, as might be predicted by the activities covered in the paired reading, the paired reading group made higher gains in skills associated with reading fluency, silent reading sentence comprehension and oral receptive language alongside comparative gains in single word reading. More surprising was their outperformance of the intervention group in writing speed and volume and their comparative gains in NC levels as the paired reading activities involved no writing tasks.

The NESSY/RR intervention has had a specific impact on spelling and phonological decoding compared with the paired reading The paired reading, with the added emphasis on oral vocabulary, comprehension strategies and positive feedback, has shown real value and produced significant gains in all aspects of literacy skills with a perhaps unexpected trade-off for writing skills. The control group had continued to make some progress in all areas of literacy. However, the failure to make significant progress in number of words written or NC levels over this 15 week period is of some concern as is the slow development of the single word reading skills

Phase two:

Analyses of the scores at the three testing points provided overall evidence of the continuing success of both the NESSY/RR and the paired reading intervention with these bilingual children, particularly at the level of word reading/decoding and vocabulary which would underpin reading comprehension. The NESSY/RR group's improvements in spelling and free writing tended to level out but the children do not regress completely.

Once the control group had completed the NESSY/RR intervention, they made significant gains with WRAT single-word reading and spelling, YARC reading rate and comprehension, vocabulary and non-word reading. However, reading and comprehension gains were marginal in terms of significance, and the gains in YARC reading accuracy/comprehension and writing speed were not significant. The picture here is more mixed.

Overall, gains from Phase One were sustained across the reading skills but remained more fragile in the area of spelling and writing when intervention was not continued.

The Participants' Perspectives.

Findings from focus groups and questionnaires completed by the TAs and SENCos emphasised the growth in the TAs' confidence in their skills and in their knowledge of the importance of the children's 'stories.

The focus groups with children, the TAs and parents from six schools emphasized the value of the project to the children. The children discussed their enjoyment of the materials used, remembering details of many books and games and the time spent with a supportive adult. Children could identify not only aspects of their reading and spelling that had improved but also how the time spent on Rapid Reading had helped them extend their vocabulary.

What the children appeared to value most was the challenging and interesting subject matter in the reading books and the 'fun' element of the spelling games supporting the emphasis on the importance of context in literacy acquisition by Gregory (1996). They loved the attention and TA's reported that their confidence and willingness to speak grew over the timescale, especially for children who were reluctant to speak initially: for example, one child had not spoken to anyone in English prior to the start of add intervention. Children started to initiate conversation and extend discussion. Parents reported changes in children's reading behaviours, for example, that they now chose to read at home and that their spelling had improved.

Some of the narrative records kept by the TAs showed development of critical thinking, increasing metacognitive awareness of strengths and difficulties in reading and spelling. Over time children talked more about their reading preferences, the nature and timing of difficulties they encountered and what helped them overcome any problems.

Most children valued the opportunity to talk about their own and each others' languages. What emerged from these discussions was the complexity of the range of languages children spoke or that were significant to the family. Often the children and parents reported use of a wider range of oral and written languages than those recorded by the schools highlighting the fact that information essential to the establishing of children's learning profiles needs to be shared more consistently between home and school. The children's perceptions and views of the programme and multi-literacies produced an unexpected and fascinating outcome – a 'snap shot' of multilingual schools and these children as global citizens, connected directly with experience of friends and family networks across the world.

Recommendations.

The following practical recommendations emerge:

- Implementing a half hour daily carefully structured intervention programme with a trained TA and two children over a period of 15 weeks can boost both reading and spelling/writing skills effectively. These improvements can be sustainable but children will need further reinforcement to automatize spelling gains;

- Care needs to be taken over selecting children to work together;

- Use of paired reading in L1 with a proficient bilingual partner, peer or adult or in L2 is highly recommended;

- Programmes should involve phonological processing, systematic and explicit teaching of new L2 phonemes supported by carefully structured multi-sensory programmes based on learners' error patterns; explicit teaching of morphology and syllable structure plus strategies for inferring meaning from context and morphology;

- ICT programmes with a strong element of fun and interest appeal but the ICT hardware must be reliable. Both Nessy and RR were endorsed by the bilingual children;

- Include explicit enrichment of vocabulary systematically linked to the literacy intervention or contextualised in some way. Emphasise building confidence in use of language and expression;

- Focus on listening and reading comprehension strategies and develop children's awareness of their own reading skills. Include explicit higher order comprehension strategies, schema work, inference work, pre-reading, prediction, SQ3R, visual and holistic approaches;

- Develop knowledge of the children's stories, knowledge of languages and literacies and ensure these enhance the teaching of literacy in English;

- Exercise caution over the need for a label or identification of risk of dyslexia in this group.

Conclusions.

In common with other studies, this project raises questions as well as enabling recommendations for the support of bilingual children experiencing difficulties in acquiring literacy. The Blatchford report (2009) had questioned the effectiveness of TA support in enhancing pupils' progress. The success of both these TA-delivered interventions, NESSY/RR and the vocabulary enriched paired reading, in raising attainment in both reading and writing, argues strongly for the deployment of TAs with small groups of bilingual children for intensive daily support over a relatively short period of time.

The sustained progress in reading related skills beyond the end of the intervention is striking. The NESSY/RR intervention, with its focus upon phoneme-grapheme mapping, word patterns and spelling skills delivered through enjoyable activities and games, was more successful than the paired reading in developing phonological awareness and spelling skills, areas particularly resistant to change in dyslexic learners (Mortimore, 2008), and it was not surprising that it should be spelling development that is less effectively sustained once the individual NESSY/

RR intervention stops. This would argue for continuing reinforcement, as recommended by all dyslexia programmes. The question arises as to whether the gains will be sustained over a longer period of time.

The project also met one of Blatchford's suggestions for improving TA effectiveness – the TAs were trained in the intervention – and the intervention was clearly signposted and structured. It is hoped that the participating schools will make full use of the enhanced skills and confidence reported by the TAs to extend their provision for these learners. The unexpected finding both of the extent of the impact of the paired reading and its spread from the expected reading skills across to writing skills also argues for further use of this economic and flexible strategy and the potential training and involvement of others within the home and school community in both L1 and L2. The benefits gained from this time spent in regular supportive communication by both the children and the TAs who worked with them are rich.

The attempt to develop an effective screener for use in identifying dyslexia risk in this group was less successful. Those children identified as at risk of dyslexia by the Lucid Dyslexia Index (LDI) were not necessarily the ones identified as at risk by the full assessment and this would support Lucid's caveat (Thomas, 2010) that LUCID/LASS were not specifically developed to identify SpLD/dyslexia. However, the data that emerged from all three screeners were described by SENCos as useful in compiling profiles of strengths and weaknesses, individualising support and increasing awareness of patterns of difference.

Issues around culture-fair assessments, use of L1, labelling and of false positive and false negative identifications of ASN in this population remain controversial and this project would dictate caution in ascribing dyslexic identity to children of this age group, particularly if they have been in UK schools for limited time. A follow up study at the end of KS3 to explore the dyslexia status of the 44 children who completed the full assessment could shed further light on this aspect.

This project has been innovative in the building of bridges between the two worlds of bilingual and dyslexia expertise and in its exploration of the impact of interventions with an under-researched group of children. Its mixed methodology design has also helped to create a richer picture of the experience of children and professionals involved in a research project and to produce a snapshot of some of our multicultural primary schools and the rich experiences, tensions and sensitivities within them. It is hoped that the findings will usefully inform both thinking about and working with these children.

References.

Alloway, T.P., Gathercole, S.E., Kirkwood, H. & Elliott, J. (2008) *The working memory rating scale: A classroom-based behavioral assessment of working memory*. London: Psychological Corporation

Baker, C. (2006) Foundations of Bilingual Education and Bilingualism (4th edition). Clevedon: Multilingual Matters

Ball, S. (2007) *The Dyslexia Checklist*. Wilts LA

Bialystok, E. (2001) Bilingualism in Development Language, Literacy and Cognition, Cambridge University Press

Blatchford, P., Bassett, P., Brown, P., Koutsoubou, M., Martin, C., Russell, A. and Webster, R., with Rubie-Davies, C. (2009) *The impact of support staff in schools*. Results from the Deployment and Impact of Support Staff project. (Strand 2 Wave 2) (DCSF-RR148). London: Department for Children, Schools and Families

Brooks, G. (2002) What works for Children with Literacy Difficulties? The Effectiveness of Intervention Schemes. University of Sheffield and DFES Research Report No 380

Crombie, M. (1997), The Effects of Specific Learning Difficulties (Dyslexia) on the Learning of a Foreign Language in School, Dyslexia, 3, pp27-47.

Crombie, M. and MacColl, H. (2001), Dyslexia and the teaching of modern foreign languages. In Peer, L. and Reid, G. (Eds.) (2001), Dyslexia-Successful Inclusion in the Secondary School, London: David Fulton

Cummins J (2000) Language. Power and Pedagogy: Bilingual Children in the Crossfire (series title: Bilingual Education and Bilingualism), Clevedon: Multilingual Matters

Durgunoglu, A.Y., Mir, M., & Ariño-Martí, S. (1993). Effects of repeated readings on bilingual and monolingual memory for text. Contemporary Educational Psychology, 18, 294-317.

Everatt, J., Ocampo,D., Kazuvire, V., Styliani, N., Smythe, I.,al Mannai, H. & Elbeheri, G. (2010) Dyslexia in Bi-scriptal readers. In N. Brunswick, S. McDougall & P. de Mornay Davies (Eds.) *Reading and dyslexia in different orthographies*. Hove: Psychology Press

Ganschow, L. and Sparks, R. (2000) 'Reflections on Foreign Language Study for Students with Language Learning Problems: Research, Issues, and Challenges', Dyslexia, 6, pp. 87-100.

Geva E., and Verhoeven, L. (2000) The Development of Second Language Reading in E. Geva & L. Verhoeven. Basic Processes in Early Second Language Reading. *Scientific Study of Reading, 4,4,261*

Hall D., Griffiths D., Haslam L. & Wilkins Y. (2001 Assessing the Needs of Bilingual Pupils: Living in Two Languages 2nd Ed. London: David Fulton

Hutchinson, JM, Whiteley, HE, Smith, CD, Connors, L (2003) The developmental progression of comprehension-related skills in children learning EAL *Journal of Research in Reading 26 (1) pp19-32*

Lipka, O., & Siegel, L.S., The Development of Reading Skills in Children with English as a Second Language. *Scientific Studies of Reading*, 11,2, 127-131

Moats, L.C. & Farrell, M.L. (2005). Multisensory structured language education in Birsh, J.R. (Ed.). *Multisensory Teaching of Basic Language Skills.* Baltimore, MD: Paul Brookes Publishing, 23-41DFE

Mortimore, T. (2008) Dyslexia and Learning Style. A Practitioner's Handbook. 2nd Edition. Chichester: Wiley

NALDIC (2011) *EAL Statistics* **http://www.naldic.org.uk/ research-and-information/eal-statistics** accessed 31.5.2012

NESSY Learning Programme (2010) Net Educational Systems Ltd **http://www.nessy.com/products.aspx**

Ott, P. (2007) Teaching Children with Dyslexia: A practical guide. London: Routledge

Rogoff, B. (2003) *The Cultural Nature of Human Development,* Oxford University Press

Rose, S. J. (2009) *Identifying and Teaching Children and Young People with Dyslexia and Literacy Difficulties: An independent report.* **www.education.gov.uk/publications/** accessed 12.09.2011

Snowling, M. J. (2010) Beyond Phonological Deficits: Sources of Individual Differences in Reading Disability. In S.A., Brady, D. Braze& C. A. Fowler (Eds.) Explaining Individual Differences in Reading. London: Psychology Press

Sparks, R. and Miller, K. (2000) Teaching a Foreign Language Using Multisensory Structured Language Techniques: Methodology and Research. *Dyslexia 6, pp. 124-132.*

Thomas, K. (2010) BDA Dyslexia and Multilingualism Project. Report on analysis of screening data. Unpublished

Turner, M. (1994) The Non-word Decoding Test. *Dyslexia Review*, 6,2, 23-24

Wolf, M. (2008) Proust and the Squid: The story and science of the reading brain. Cambridge: Icon Books

Ziegler, J. C., & Goswami, U. C. (2005). Reading acquisition, developmental dyslexia and skilled reading across languages: A psycholinguistic grain size theory. *Psychological Bulletin, 131(1), 3-29.[pdf]*

The Dyslexia and Multilingualism team

Bath Spa University: Anny Northcote, Mim Hutchings, Lynda Hansen, Carrie Ansell

Canterbury Christ Church University, New Zealand: Consultant: John Everatt

BDA: Kate Saunders, Liz Horobin, Jill Fernando

Thanks to: Melanie Nind, Pearson, NESSY and Kevin Thomas and Rik Leedale of Lucid Research

Chapter 5 – Dyslexia and Multilingualism: A case study.

Jill Fernando.

Introduction.

In her chapter, "Identifying and supporting literacy acquisition in bilingual learners potentially at risk of dyslexia: The Big Lottery Dyslexia and Multilingualism Project", Dr Mortimore provided a detailed explanation of the Dyslexia and Multilingualism Project and presented an overview of the findings. This section will now narrow the focus and present the reader with a sense of how the project was experienced in one school.

C Primary School was selected for a case study as it embraced the project with enthusiasm from the start. It was one of the relatively few schools that engaged teacher support by adopting a whole school approach and ensuring that teachers were aware of the project from the outset. In addition, the staff who took part in the project were passionate about supporting dyslexic children and were committed to capitalising on their increased knowledge and new materials to offer a programme of support to a greater number of children once the project was completed.

The school has around 450 pupils, about 80% of whom come from a minority ethnic background. Most pupils have English as an additional language. Pupils of Pakistani origin comprise over half the number of pupils at the school. The local authority had recommended that the school participate because of its high numbers

of children with English as an Additional Language.
The project coordinator had therefore contacted the
school directly and received a very positive response.

School staff involved in the project.

The Special Educational Needs Coordinator (SENCo) was
interested in taking part in the project because she had
a long-standing interest in dyslexia and had an ambition
to establish a dyslexia-friendly school. She had been a
SENCo for 4 years and also fulfilled the role of acting head
when the head teacher was away from school. Her first
task was to select 2 Teaching Assistants (TAs) who would
be responsible for delivering the paired reading and the
main intervention. She selected W for her experience of
working with dyslexic children and F for her multilingual
knowledge. W was a particularly experienced TA who
had worked in the field for 21 years and had received
training in disability, diversity, Special Educational
Needs, dyslexia and working with bilingual learners.

Project training.

The SENCo took part in a day's project training at the
beginning of September 2010. This training was led by
staff from Bath Spa University and the British Dyslexia
Association and included information about the research
project itself and training in the use of the screening and
testing materials. W and F attended two days project training.
This training was again delivered by Bath Spa and BDA
staff and it provided information about the project, input
on both dyslexia and multilingualism and training on the
implementation of the intervention materials. In addition,

Pearson Heinemann provided an overview of their product, Rapid Reading, which was to be used during the intervention.

The screening process.

The SENCo and TAs then selected 12 children who they felt were 'not thriving' in terms of their literacy skills. The children completed the Lucid LASS Assessment System (containing 8 computerised tests) and a verbal reasoning test on Lucid Ability. A dyslexia checklist was completed for each child and the class teachers completed a questionnaire on classroom behaviours. Staff from Bath Spa University and the BDA looked at all the information and results and selected children who seemed to display dyslexic indicators. Two of these children had scored poorly on the literacy tests despite having good scores on the non verbal reasoning test. The third child had scored well on visual memory but poorly on the literacy tests and auditory memory. The fourth child scored very poorly on non word decoding but performed relatively well on visual and auditory memory.

Project structure.

In order to facilitate reciprocal support and enable TAs to share experiences, C Primary School and 2 other nearby schools were selected as Group B schools. This meant that after the initial testing had been carried out, the TAs would run a 15 week 'alternative intervention' of paired reading. The children would then be re-tested and the TAs would run the 15 week intervention programme using Nessy and Rapid Reading. Each intervention would be carried out for half an hour a day with each TA working with two children. After the intervention, the children would be tested again.

A whole school approach.

The SENCo ensured that other staff were made aware of the project by organising a staff meeting in which she and W gave some information about dyslexia, explained about the project and encouraged staff to ask questions. One teacher subsequently came to observe a session on Nessy. Other teachers identified children that they thought might be dyslexic and requested W to screen them. The project raised staff's awareness of dyslexia and appears to have been viewed in a very positive light.

The paired reading experience.

W and F were allocated a separate room to run the paired reading intervention and they were able to operate without disturbances. A positive routine was established very early on. The children enjoyed being able to bring a book from home or to select a book from school. Each child was also allowed to select a magazine on an area of interest. At the end of each session, the children were encouraged to look at a big poster displaying a huge range of adjectives and to decide which one best reflected how they were feeling.

W commented that one child had initially made a lot of omissions and substitutions but, as the paired reading progressed, she slowed down her pace and her reading became more accurate. W reported that all the children got into the habit of self-correcting during the paired reading and that they all made discernible progress. She said that the strategy of asking the child to knock when they wanted to speak or stop speaking worked really well and that one of the children continues to use this method a year later.

The project coordinator observed the paired reading and saw examples of self-correction. The children seemed keen and motivated. Both TAs engaged the children in discussion about the books, exploited the pictures and provided good explanations of vocabulary using clear examples.

The main intervention.

As was the case in several other schools, unforeseen circumstances meant that a TA was unable to remain on the project. F became pregnant and because she would have been unable to carry out the whole intervention, the SENCo requested for her to be replaced by another TA, K. The SENCo recognised that K had not participated in the initial training but felt that with support from W and from the project coordinator, K would be able to run the intervention with 2 children without having a negative effect on the integrity of the project. W and K both attended a TA meeting prior to the main intervention and K was able to familiarise herself with the intervention materials.

In addition, one of the TAs from a Group A school who had carried out the intervention in Phase 1 offered to visit the school and help W and K start the intervention. She helped them install the software, showed them how to determine at which level each child should start and advised them how to complete the paperwork. The project coordinator followed this up with visits to the school, observing K, offering guidance and answering any outstanding questions.

W said that she felt quite confident at the start of the intervention. She thought that it had been beneficial to start with the paired reading as a routine had been established and she knew the reading level of the children. In addition, her SENCo allowed her an additional 15 minutes each day to enable her to set up at the beginning and monitor at the end. This meant that the full 30 minutes were devoted to the intervention. W and K made up any missed sessions either by doing additional sessions or, occasionally by doing longer sessions. By the end of the intervention, they had completed the maximum number of sessions (75) with all the children. This situation was by no means typical. Most schools did not formally allocate additional time to their TAs. Although some TAs were able to remain out of class for more than half an hour due to the goodwill and flexibility of the teachers to whom they were assigned, others were required to adhere to the official timings. This meant that setting up encroached on the intervention time and TAs were unable to monitor the children's work at the end of a session. In most cases, sessions that were missed were not re-scheduled.

W reported that the children enjoyed the Rapid Reading books. She said it worked better if the children read to her, then did a worksheet and went on the Rapid Reading Assistant later – this is a software feature that enables a child to listen to a text being read and to record themselves reading the text. She said that all the children really enjoyed playing back their recordings and listening to themselves and that this appeared to act as a motivating factor. Unlike a significant number of other schools, W and K did not experience any significant technical problems with the software or the microphones.

The project coordinator observed several sessions during the intervention and the children always seemed motivated and enthusiastic. The TAs established a good balance between Nessy and Rapid Reading and included reinforcement activities such as Rainbow Writing in which the children practised spellings by writing a word in cursive script in one colour and then going over the writing several times in different colours.

W observed that the children, all four of whom are Muslim, had been shocked by the references to pigs, pork and ham on the Nessy worksheets. Their reaction is probably due to the fact that the eating of pork and touching of pigs is forbidden in the Islamic religion. When the project coordinator raised this issue at another school, a Muslim TA said that the inclusion of pigs on worksheets was not offensive. However, whatever the official stance, it is clearly an area of sensitivity.

Apart from this, the children all loved the Nessy software and enjoyed the reward system which enabled them to accumulate nuggets which could later be spent at the fair! W also commented that although the children had enjoyed doing Rainbow Writing, they had preferred using the sand tray which enabled them to spell out words in sand and suited a kinaesthetic/tactile learning style. On one occasion, they had used an alphabet arc but she felt that the children had found it 'babyish'.

W felt that all four children improved significantly but found it difficult to pinpoint whether the improvements occurred mainly during the paired reading or during the intervention. In the mid project testing, all four children showed improvements in non word decoding and three out of four of the children had made even bigger improvements by the time of the final testing. All four children improved between the initial and mid-project testing on the WRAT sentence comprehension and had continued to make progress up to the final testing. Three out of four of the children showed a big improvement between the initial and mid-project testing on the YARC reading comprehension and all four improved during the intervention. Three out of four of the children's age equivalent scores on receptive vocabulary (BPVS3) improved by over a year (between October and July) with one children progressing from 6:00 to 8:05.

All of the children's reading accuracy (YARC) improved by a minimum of a year with two children improving by more than two years. The pattern of spelling results was less consistent but three out of four of the children scored better in the final testing than the initial testing (standard scores increasing from 87 to 93, 80 to 93, and 87 to 91). The same three children also scored better in the final testing of single word reading (standard scores increasing from 80 to 87, 80 to 93, and 87 to 97). The fourth child scored lower in the final testing on the spelling and only made a slight improvement in single word reading.

Asked whether she would make any changes to the structure of the intervention, W said that she thought that it might be better to use the Nessy software for a week and then Rapid Reading for a week. She felt that asking the children to work simultaneously on spelling rules and reading comprehension was too onerous and amounted to giving them 'two lots of business' at the same time. But, unlike some TAs in other schools, she did not experience any difficulties running the intervention with two children at the same time.

Project as a springboard to further studies/ involvement in the field of dyslexia.

W was extremely enthusiastic about the project and its impact on the children. This enthusiasm and increased confidence motivated her to take part in the BDA Shine Project. This comprises weekly after school workshops for children with dyslexic-type difficulties. W supports the children with reading, writing, maths and touch typing. She has also continued her professional development and is currently following a Level 3 BDA training programme on dyslexia.

Post-project activities.

The children completed their intervention in July 2011. Once the school had re-tested the children, their involvement in the project concluded; however, they were able to retain the testing and intervention materials to use as they wished. In September 2011, W began working with 20 children on Nessy and this number had increased to 30 by November. The materials are no longer restricted to children with English as an Additional Language but, interestingly, only 4 of the 30 children are monolingual. The class teachers provide targets, for example 'ie' or 'ew' spellings and W identifies the appropriate lesson in Nessy. W works for an hour with 6 children, 3 working on computers and 3 on Nessy worksheets. The children swap around after 30 minutes. Each child receives two one hour sessions which also include multisensory reinforcement with the use of Rainbow Writing and the sandtray. When worksheets have been completed, W gives them to the teachers who re-visit the worksheets again a week later with the children in order to reinforce the learning. W reports positive feedback from class teachers.

When the project started, W mentioned a child who staff believed to be dyslexic. The screening process also indicated a strong likelihood of dyslexia with high scores on non verbal reasoning, an average score on verbal reasoning but poor scores on auditory memory and on the literacy and diagnostic tests. As part of the project's aim to evaluate the screening tools, this child was selected for a full assessment of literacy skills, carried out by an external assessor. The assessor found that relative to her high ability scores, there were weaknesses in spelling, reading and listening comprehension and in short term auditory memory. The assessor concluded that the child showed some signs of a dyslexic profile. The school arranged for one of its bilingual TAs to interpret so that the father could receive feedback on his daughter's assessment.

This child's mid-project testing results showed great improvement in sentence comprehension (WRAT4) with her standard score increasing from 69 to 82. Her text comprehension as measured by the YARC progressed from an age equivalent score of 6 years, 5 months to 7 years, 8 months. Her reading accuracy improved from 6 years, 2 months to 7 years, one month. Her score on the Non Words also improved from 13/39 to 17/39.

The final testing showed a great improvement in non word decoding with a raw score of 29/39 and in text comprehension (YARC) with an age equivalent score of 8 years, 10 months. Sentence comprehension improved at a steadier rate (standard score rising from

82 to 87) as did reading accuracy (age equivalent score rising from 7 years 1 month to 7 years 6 months).

Unlike the other 3 children, this child did not show improvement in single word spelling (WRAT4) and her improvements on single word reading (WRAT4) and receptive vocabulary (BPVS3) were slight.

Conclusion.

This case study illustrates the potential effectiveness of TA-led interventions conducted with the full backing of senior staff and class teachers. It demonstrates the improvements that multilingual children can make when working 2:1 on a daily basis on a structured multisensory programme in a safe and non threatening environment.

Tests used in pre, mid and post intervention testing and in screening process

WRAT4 Single Word Reading, Single Word Spelling and Sentence Comprehension (Wide Range Achievement Test 4(2006), Wide Range Inc.)

The Nonword Decoding Test, Turner (2003)

The British Picture Vocabulary Scale (BPVSIII) (2009) GL Assessment Ltd)

York Assessment of Reading for Comprehension (YARC) (2009) GL Assessment

Lucid LASS Junior (8-11), Lucid Research Ltd

Lucid Ability (7-12) (verbal reasoning only), Lucid Research Ltd

Dyslexia Checklist adapted from Wesford (Ball 2007)

Working Memory Rating Scale (Alloway *et al.*, 2008)

Chapter 6 – Assistive Technology for the Multilingual Dyslexic Individual.

Professor Ian Smythe.

The purpose of this chapter is to identify the issues that are confronted by the multilingual dyslexic individual, and show how they may be addressed creatively to support those areas of difficulty. Due to the rapidly evolving nature of technology, as well as the diversity of languages and abilities encountered, there can be no definitive list of recommended software. Instead this chapter will identify uses, suggest possible solutions and use a case study to show how technology can be used in different ways. It is for the reader to decide how the ideas can be adapted to their specific needs.

In order to be visually (dyslexia) friendly, this chapter is mapped out as a concept map, to indicate the relationship between topics, and what will be appearing.

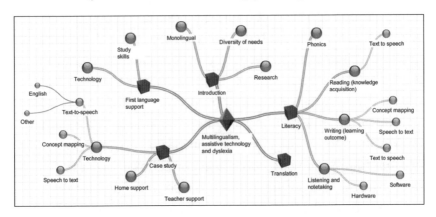

Introduction.

To state that every multilingual dyslexic individual has their own unique set of strengths and weaknesses is to state the obvious. Yet ironically, despite the diversity that each individual may bring to the learning environment, the core assistive technology tools are very few, and to a large extend, those same tools will suit most multilingual dyslexic individuals. But it is not what the tools are, but how they are utilised that is the key. It is the potential to use the technology in different ways that will be explored here.

The core symptoms of dyslexia are a difficulty in (the acquisition of) fluent and accurate reading and writing skills. Therefore, any technology that can support these skills will be seen to be of benefit to these individuals. However, whilst in many areas (such as phonics teaching) it is relatively easy to demonstrate the efficacy of any methodology through thorough research, in the case of multilingual dyslexic individuals, it is more difficult to find a representative homogenous cohort that could be used for studying. (For example, if you wanted to know what would be the expected spelling ability of a Chinese child in Year 9 who arrived in the UK four years ago, speaks Chinese at home with their parents, but English with their friends and watches English TV, you would need to find another 100 kids with the same background to create a reliable comparison!)Therefore, much of what follows may be considered anecdotal. However, the author would suggest that it is also only anecdotal evidence that says look both ways before crossing the road!

It will become apparent that the technology may also be useful for non-dyslexic multilingual individuals. This is true. However, the dyslexic individuals will be looking to support from the technology long after the non-dyslexic individuals have stopped using it. This point is important, since it illustrates that the access to the technology does not confer an unfair advantage to its users.

There are a number of approaches that could be used to identify useful assistive technologies for multilingual dyslexic individuals, such as technology categories (hardware, software, interfaces etc – (See Smythe, 2010). However, it may be more appropriate here to consider the desirable outcome. To put it another way, what is the nature of the difficulties, and what possibilities exist to support those difficulties. The key areas to consider are:

- Phonics
- Reading and writing
- Listening and note-taking
- Additional knowledge acquisition

Phonics.

Phonics means different things to different people. But here we refer to the acquisition of all those skills that support reading and writing, including sound segmentation skills (rhyming, alliteration etc), sound blending, and sound-letter correspondence. The nature and importance of these different components of skill deficits in multilingual dyslexic individuals is discussed elsewhere in this book. Therefore, the intention is merely to identify some ways that could be used to support multilingual individuals using technology.

Technology should not be seen as the solution, but as a tool that can be used by creative teachers. There is no software especially for these individuals since the skills, abilities and language backgrounds are so diverse. However, the basic rule is that what is good for dyslexic individuals is also good for non-dyslexic individuals, with the caveat that if they know the word used for practice, there is a much better chance of retention/learning.

Listening to sounds in context will help considerably with the ability to identify and distinguish between sounds, especially if the listener can also recognize the subtle differences between sounds such as b/p and f/v. Listening to stories is a good start, provided the vocabulary is age-appropriate. This can be problematic, since "easy vocabulary" stories are usually written for younger children. If no appropriate pre-recorded commercial or free online stories can be found, you may consider, for example, recording the reading of a book yourself, and which the pupil may then listen to. Another alternative is to type out exercises and have them read by text to speech technology. Further reinforcement can be gained if the person can also see the text highlighted as it is read if the speed is appropriate. However, be careful that the reader does not compromise comprehension when following the highlighter.

Due care and attention should be made to ensure the vocabulary set is appropriate. A good starting point for the early language learner is Charles Ogden's 850 Basic English words (**http://ogden.basic-english.org/**) that allow the user to express 90 per cent of their ideas.

Although now a little dated, if does provide a more useful guide than simply word frequency lists.

When it comes to correct pronunciation, there is little that can replace the informed teacher and/or parent. Creative use of software such as Audacity (free open source recording software) or specialist software such as Chatback (available from Xavier Educational Software) may help. But probably the most likely way forward in the next few years is through intelligent use of motivating software, such as the Google tablets and iPhone with their built in speech-to-text. Although not as accurate as dedicated trainable text-to-speech, their high motivational levels offers the potential to inspire kids to improve their speaking skills.

There are a number of software packages available that are used to help with basic phonics for monolingual dyslexic pupils. These may be utilised, but should not be seen as suitable unless a teacher is working closely with the pupil.

Another area that should not be ignored is handwriting. Despite the ubiquitous nature of the computer, handwriting is still very important. If the individual comes from a background where a totally different script is used (such as Arabic or Chinese), then they may not have the fine motor patterns needed to produce good (or even readable) handwriting. Again, Apple, Google and Samsung phablets are increasingly available as a tool that can be utilised to practice those skills using handwriting recognition software as an instant metric for the skill.

There are also many typing courses available, and they may be useful, provided the reading age of the target words is not too high. Note that typing is often seen as helping to develop "spelling engrams", that is patterns in the brain that allow us to type a word quickly without thinking about what keys to press. This again offers a reinforcement tool.

Reading and writing.

Reading is often seen as extracting meaning from written text, increasingly presented on the screen rather than in paper versions. It may also be considered as the acquisition of other peoples thoughts and ideas, or checking your own (written) thoughts. Conversely, writing is about putting thoughts into a written format, which by convention is continuous text. However, it may also be in other forms such as concept maps.

There are a number of circumstances where the technology can remove the reading difficulty by providing auditory versions of written text. These include

- Reading an electronic document (Word, pdf etc)
- Reading text on the internet
- Reading online and offline e-books
- Proofreading your own work
- Reading email and chat
- Hearing how some English words are pronounced correctly
- Producing mp3 files to download and listen to later.

This list is true for all dyslexic individuals, and needs little explanation. (See Smythe 2010 for further information.) How this will be applied to a specific multilingual individuals will depend upon the individual, but there are many times when an individual may have poor reading skills but their spoken English is adequate to understand. Provision of text-to-speech software opens up the possibility of acquiring knowledge and not being restricted to the limits of their reading ability. This approach will depend on the access of material such as teachers notes. Email, USB memory sticks and shared areas (e.g. Dropbox) are just three ways where the material can be send to the student.

Another area where text-to-speech software can be of great help is when proof reading one's own work. All too often an individual will read what they think is there rather than what is actually there. Text-to-speech removes this problem, and will allow the individual to hear what is actually written.

From a technology perspective, the two types of software to consider are:

- Tool bar type
- Cut and paste

Tool bar text-to-speech software can be used with all types of files including Microsoft Word documents, web pages and email. The most common commercial versions are ClaroRead and Texthelp. Both come as installable software and the type that can be run from a USB stick. There are now many voices and language versions, but you will need to check with the specific software you choose as to what works with that particular tool. Like most software, most text-to-speech software have trial versions.

Cut and paste software is the type where material has to be pasted into the work area of the software.

This type is usually free, but restricted to poor quality voices. One version of note is Balabolka, which is open source and can be used with commercial voices or the free (low quality) Microsoft voices. Commercial high quality voices may be purchased separately for as little as £30. (See the table on voices for what is available.)

When it comes to writing, the process may be considered as two parts:

- Mapping it out
- Writing the essay

Mapping it out refers to taking ideas and writing them down in a way that can apply structure, but without writing out the whole document. Concept maps (sometimes known as mind maps or spider diagrams) are the most common tool. Again, how they are used with the multilingual dyslexic individual will depend upon the specific needs and current skill levels. But one approach to consider is as follows:

Step One.

Ask the individual to map out (using techniques described elsewhere) the "idea" (e.g. essay), in their preferred language.

Step Two.

Ask them to translate it into English

Step Three.

Review and discuss their English language used for the map and how this may need to be adjusted. This will help their ability to research that subject matter, as well as improve their vocabulary.

From a software perspective, there are many commercial options available, and several free versions. Xmind is a very sophisticated offline open source package, which has the advantage of having all the options you may need and as you would expect in commercial packages. However, the provision of many options in drop down menus and libraries often serves only to distract from the real task in hand. Simpler options that allow you to focus on the task (and not have to worry about the meaning of what is in the dropdown menu) can be found in online software such as Iconmaps (**www.iconmap.com**).

Having developed the map, a process of review and support can be used to develop the concept map into flowing text.

Unfortunately for homework it is difficult to guard against the use of translation tools such as Google Translate, with all its built in errors, and it taking away any potential to learn. In the classroom, simple electronic dictionaries can be useful, either as hand-held or computer-based. However, be careful of the temptation to buy the best, as they will often show lots of options for misspelled words, and the pupil is left bewildered as to which option to choose.

Teaching the use of spellcheckers in word processors is obvious. But many people forget to provide adequate instructions for using grammar checkers. Software such as Microsoft Word has built in grammar checkers which will help to correct many small issues. This is not always available in other language versions and therefore the student may be familiar with the software in their preferred language, but not know about grammar checkers. Therefore a quick guide as to their use is often advantageous. There are also many online grammar checkers that can help with this. (Try "online grammar checker" in your search engine.)

A brief mention should be made of speech-to-text since it is part of the writing process for many dyslexic individuals. While this is good for the monolingual English pupil, it is of limited use to those whose pronunciation is a long way from "standard" English. It is possible to train the software, and in some cases, even with a strong non-native pronunciation, it may be advantageous to use. But it will be very important to ensure that training is carried out in full, and that the ability to adapt it to the voice of the user is full realised. Unfortunately the range of languages for speech to text is very limited.

Listening and notetaking.

Listening and notetaking at the same time can be a tricky task for any individual. But if you are not only trying to process for meaning while listening but also having to translate, the difficulties are magnified. For this reason, some form of recording device is recommended.

There are many types of digital sound recorders available, including standalone devices, smart phones, phablets and tools loaded onto laptops. Their uses include:

- To record lessons or key parts of lessons
- To say aloud ideas before you forget them
- To record the homework
- To remember instructions
- Communicating between home and school

The downside to this technology is that one still has to remember that it has limitations and it is easy to trust the technology only for it to fail at a key moment. The ability to use the information will depend not only upon where and how it is used, but also the quality of the microphone (don't forget that a directional mic may be required), remembering to download the content of the digital recorder regularly, and the battery life!

The key is not only in having the recording but also how to extract notes from it. There are many types of annotation software available. Audio Notetaker (by Sonocent) is just one of many options that can be found on the internet. However, to reiterate, it is how the technology is used, rather than the technology itself, that will help overcome the particular difficulty. For example, the teacher may want to check the annotations of the student to ensure they have an appropriate understanding of those lessons.

Additional knowledge acquisition and translation.

As well as working on specific text, students are encouraged to self-research and review material in books and on the internet. Depending on their language skills, it may be appropriate to use technology to help this process. For example, using text-to-speech in the preferred language (where available – see later section) may facilitate knowledge acquisition, allow them to understand the principles in more depth than may be available in their first language, and then re-tell it in English using words that are familiar to them.

Clearly, without supervision, Google Translate, either in the cut and paste form or translating a whole website at once (see the guide to Google Translate as to how to do that), is the easy option. Although it is impossible to ban its use, if the user has a clear understanding of the limitation, then there are circumstances where this can be a useful tool.

There are a number of pieces of software that have the ability to assist with translation at the word level, such as ClaroLingo. This uses technology to allow you to hover over a word and have an instant translation and, where available, have it spoken in another language. This can be very useful if a single word is not known, or there is uncertainty as to how to pronounce it.

First language support.

It is always a problem to decide if you should encourage more study in the English language, or allow the pupil to go off to work in their own language. Clearly there are many circumstances where knowledge acquisition in the first language will provide greater opportunity for the individual to limit how far they fall behind in the classroom. The following provides a list of the languages available for text-to-speech. Due care and attention has to be taken, since not all are available to the general public, and they may not be compatible with all software. But it does provides a good indication of what is out there.

Language	MS Free	Acapela	AT&T	Cepstral	CereProc	Ivona	Loquendo	RealSpeak
Arabic		Yes					Yes	
Chinese - Cantonese								Yes
Chinese - Mandarin							Yes	Yes
Czech		Yes						Yes
Danish		Yes					Yes	Yes
Dutch	Yes	Yes					Yes	Yes
English	Yes	Yes	Yes	Yes	Yes	Yes	Yes	Yes
Finnish		Yes					Yes	Yes
French	Yes	Yes	Yes	Yes	Yes	Yes	Yes	Yes
German	Yes	Yes	Yes	Yes	Yes	Yes	Yes	Yes
Greek		Yes					Yes	Yes
Hindi								Yes
Italian	Yes	Yes	Yes	Yes		Yes	Yes	Yes
Japanese	Yes				Yes			Yes
Korean	Yes							Yes
Norwegian		Yes					Yes	Yes
Polish		Yes				Yes	Yes	
Portuguese	Yes	Yes					Yes	Yes
Romanian						Yes		Yes
Russian	Yes	Yes					Yes	Yes
Spanish	Yes	Yes	Yes	Yes	Yes	Yes	Yes	Yes
Swedish		Yes					Yes	Yes
Thai								Yes
Turkish		Yes					Yes	Yes
Welsh						Yes		

Concept mapping tools are available in many languages. However, as previously mentioned, if may be best to use one with few menus, and therefore language is not so important. Speech-to-text, as mentioned previously, is available in a few European languages, but few others.

First language support – Study Skills.

Study skills have become common place in the support of the dyslexic individual. However, it can be difficult to find material in the first language which they can access. The following is a compilation from various EU funded projects which offer resources that may be helpful for teachers, for teaching assistants (especially if they are language support) and importantly, for students themselves. Please note that all of these listed are free and available online.

Language	Who for	Resource
English (EN)	Students	Study skills book for student (Dessdys)
		Self-assessment tool for the dyslexic student (Dyslexia Veto)
		Self-assessment tool (Embed)
		Self-help e-book (Embed)
		Self-assessment tool for the dyslexic student (iSheds)
		Self-support e-book for dyslexic students (iSheds)
	Tutors and institutions	Training material for lecturers and those supporting dyslexic students (Adystrain)
		Dyslexia Quality Mark (Dyslexia Veto)
		Institution-wide assessment tool (Dyslexia Veto)
		Technology needs and audit tool for individuals (Embed)
		Technology needs and audit tool for institutions (Embed)
		Technology needs and audit tool for support workers (Embed)
		E-book for those who support dyslexic students (iSheds)
		Guide to supporting multilingual students (DysLang)
Bosnian (BA)	Students	Self-support e-book for dyslexic students (iSheds)
	Tutors and institutions	E-book for those who support dyslexic students (iSheds)
		Policy reviews and checklists (iSheds)

Language	Who for	Resource
Bulgarian (BG)	Students	Study skills book for student (Dessdys)
		Self-assessment tool for the dyslexic student (Dyslexia Veto)
		Self-help e-book (Embed)
	Tutors and institutions	Dyslexia Quality Mark (Dyslexia Veto)
		Technology needs and audit tool for individuals (Embed)
		Technology needs and audit tool for institutions (Embed)
		Technology needs and audit tool for support workers (Embed)
		Guide to supporting multilingual students (DysLang)
Croatian (HR)	Students	Self-assessment tool for the dyslexic student (iSheds)
		Self-support e-book for dyslexic students (iSheds)
		Free online Concept Mapping (iSheds)
		Free online Reminders system (iSheds)
	Tutors and institutions	E-book for those who support dyslexic students (iSheds)
		Policy reviews and checklists (iSheds)
Czech (CZ)	Tutors	Guide to supporting multilingual students (DysLang)
Danish (DK)	Tutors	Training material for lecturers and those supporting dyslexic students (Adystrain)
Finnish (FI)	Tutors	Training material for lecturers and those supporting dyslexic students (Adystrain)
German (AU/DE)	Tutors	Training material for lecturers and those supporting dyslexic students (Adystrain)
Greek (EL)	Students	Self help e-book (Include)

Language	Who for	Resource
Hungarian (HU)	Students	Study skills book for student (Dessdys)
		Self-help e-book (Embed)
		Self-support e-book for dyslexic students (iSheds)
	Tutors and institutions	Training material for lecturers and those supporting dyslexic students (Adystrain)
		Dyslexia Quality Mark (Dyslexia Veto)
		Institution-wide assessment tool (Dyslexia Veto)
		Technology needs and audit tool for individuals (Embed)
		Technology needs and audit tool for institutions (Embed)
		Technology needs and audit tool for support workers (Embed)
		E-book for those who support dyslexic students (iSheds)
		Policy reviews and checklists (iSheds)
Italian (IT)	Students	Study skills book for student (Dessdys)
		Self-help e-book (Embed)
	Tutors and institutions	Dyslexia Quality Mark (Dyslexia Veto)
		Institution-wide assessment tool (Dyslexia Veto)
		Technology needs and audit tool for individuals (Embed)
		Technology needs and audit tool for institutions (Embed)
		Technology needs and audit tool for support workers (Embed)
		Guide to supporting multilingual students (DysLang)
Polish (PL)	Students	Self-help e-book (Embed)
	Tutors and institutions	Technology needs and audit tool for individuals (Embed)
		Technology needs and audit tool for institutions (Embed)
		Technology needs and audit tool for support workers (Embed)

Language	Who for	Resource
Romanian (RO)	Students	Self-support e-book for dyslexic students (iSheds)
	Tutors and institutions	Dyslexia Quality Mark (Dyslexia Veto)
		Institution-wide assessment tool (Dyslexia Veto)
		E-book for those who support dyslexic students (iSheds)
		Policy reviews and checklists (iSheds)
Serbian(RS)	Students	Self-support e-book for dyslexic students (iSheds)
	Tutors and institutions	E-book for those who support dyslexic students (iSheds)
		Policy reviews and checklists (iSheds)
Slovenian (SI)	Students	Self-support e-book for dyslexic students (iSheds)
	Tutors and institutions	E-book for those who support dyslexic students (iSheds)
		Policy reviews and checklists (iSheds)
Spanish (ES)	Students	Self-help e-book (Embed)
	Tutors and institutions	Training material for lecturers and those supporting dyslexic students (Adystrain)
		Technology needs and audit tool for individuals (Embed)
		Technology needs and audit tool for institutions (Embed)
		Technology needs and audit tool for support workers (Embed)
Turkish (TR)	Students	Study skills book for student (Dessdys)
	Tutors	Guide to supporting multilingual students (DysLang)

Case study – Mikolaj from Poland.

One of the largest language groups in the UK is Polish, with an estimated 619,000 Polish nationals residents in the United Kingdom. There are currently no collated statistics to say how many are at school, and a lack of due process means we cannot be sure of how many Polish dyslexic individuals there are. But a conservative estimate suggests that there would be 5,000 Polish dyslexic pupils in the UK. So let us take one case study and see how technology could help.

Mikolaj is 12 years old, and has been in the UK for five years. The school think his problem is that he speaks Polish at home, and is confused by attending a Polish school on Saturday where he practices his Polish literacy skills. His parents had an assessment in Poland through the Polish Dyslexia Association, which confirmed his dyslexia. The school will not release extra resources, but they do allow him to use the technology that his parents have supplied. The primary assistive technologies can be summarised as:

Text to speech – Where possible Mikolaj uses text-to-speech at school, using ClaroRead with a Polish voice. At home he uses Balabolka, a cut-and paste type, for which his parents bought a high quality voice online. They also use it to help with notes from school.

Concept mapping – Online Ikonmap (**www.ikonmap.com**) has been found to be very useful as it is simple and easy to use. The teacher found that he was too easily distracted when using softare with too many options.

Speech to text – The English language Dragon Naturally Speaking is proving problematic to train, but his parents are trying to assist him. However, Mikolaj has started to use the Polish version – Skyrbot – for the rare occasions when he does write in Polish.

Homework is facilitated using the technology in various ways. Concept maps are usually used to plan out ideas in three stages: 1) First language, 2) His version in English, 3) Teacher moderated English. The final version is then outputted to Word before writing it out in full. A handheld translator is used to check single words and Claro is used to speak on a word by word basis as he is typing since he has reasonable spoken English but poor written English, with some confusion over letters that have different sounds in English. He has learned to use spellchecker to his advantage, but does not use auto-replace as he understands that this would cause long term problems. He finds the grammar checker difficult to understand, and tends to just accept the Word suggestion each time. This causes some problems with teachers.

Teachers accept that they cannot monitor his use of technology at home, and his French homework "is better than expected." His errors are very similar to those that Google Translate would make.

He has an email address which the school uses to communicate with the home, and where his homework is sent. His parents have access to that address, which helps them check he has the right homework and deadlines.

Conclusion.

The success of the software as a support tool will not depend so much on the software itself, but the way in which it is used. New technology comes out on a regular basis. But the answer is not the technology or about money. A piece of software itself will not solve an issue – it only provides the potential to overcome the problem. Do not underestimate training, especially if it can be augmented with YouTube videos. (Here is a tip – Ask the pupil to prepare a short video or ppt on how to use a piece of assistive software as you have another pupil that needs to use it.

This can be a highly motivating way to help them learn how to use it effectively!)

Finally, try to think very carefully about the specific use of the software, rather than the generic use. For example, it is easy to make an mp3 of a book chapter. But how do you rewind to hear the last paragraph that you did not quite understand? (Author's choice: I use Balabolka with a commercial voice, and use their controls to have one sound file for each paragraph, so I can go back in small steps.)

Free does not mean less quality. I have not yet found a concept map tool that is better than the simple free version to be found at **www.ikonmap.com**. It is its simplicity that appeals to me. But you can usually download a trial version of most software which offers opportunities to compare.

Remember that training is everything. Do not assume that you, as the teacher/supporter have full knowledge of the latest versions. And some background research on YouTube could be more useful than trying to read an instruction manual.

Be creative: Powerpoint can be used for concept maps, and smart phones as recording devices. And if the individual is really stuck on something, they could always take a snap on their phone, send the photo, and say "What does this mean?"

And finally, involve the individual in the process. When it comes to the technology, they may find more solutions than you!

Dr Smythe is Visiting Professor at the School of Education, University of Wales, Newport, writes extensively about dyslexia and assistive technology and is author of "Dyslexia in the Digital Age" published by Continuum. He may be contacted at **ianssmythe@gmail.com**

References and further reading.

There are no books that cover this subject adequately. However the following resources may be of interest, including some that are about teaching languages to native English speakers. Again, the ideas within the books may be adapted creatively for many multilingual dyslexic individuals.

Books.

Kormos J and Smith AM (2012) *Teaching Languages to Students with Specific Learning Differences*. Multimedia Matters. Bristol

Marsh D (2005) *Special Educational Needs in Europe. The teaching and learning of Foreign Languages*. European Commission. Brussels

Schneider E and Crombie M (2003) *Dyslexia and Modern Foreign languages. British Dyslexia Association*. Reading.

Smythe I (2010) *Dyslexia in the digital age*. Continuum Books. London

Smythe I, Everatt J and Salter R (2004) *International Book of Dyslexia – A Cross-Language Comparison and Practice Guide* (Second edition). Wileys. Chichester

Dyslang (**www.dyslang.eu**) An EU project about supporting multilingual dyslexic pupils learn an additional language.

For a list of resource links in this chapter, please visit
www.doitprofiler.net/resources/languages